Integrated Measurement – KPIs and Metrics for ITSM

A narrative account

Integrated Measurement – KPIs and Metrics for ITSM

A narrative account

DANIEL McLEAN

IT Governance Publishing

Every possible effort has been made to ensure that the information contained in this book is accurate at the time of going to press, and the publisher and the author cannot accept responsibility for any errors or omissions, however caused. Any opinions expressed in this book are those of the author, not the publisher. Websites identified are for reference only, not endorsement, and any website visits are at the reader's own risk. No responsibility for loss or damage occasioned to any person acting, or refraining from action, as a result of the material in this publication can be accepted by the publisher or the author.

Apart from any fair dealing for the purposes of research or private study, or criticism or review, as permitted under the Copyright, Designs and Patents Act 1988, this publication may only be reproduced, stored or transmitted, in any form, or by any means, with the prior permission in writing of the publisher or, in the case of reprographic reproduction, in accordance with the terms of licenses issued by the Copyright Licensing Agency. Enquiries concerning reproduction outside those terms should be sent to the publishers at the following address:

IT Governance Publishing
IT Governance Limited
Unit 3, Clive Court
Bartholomew's Walk
Cambridgeshire Business Park
Ely
Cambridgeshire
CB7 4EA
United Kingdom

www.itgovernance.co.uk

First published in the United Kingdom in 2013
by IT Governance Publishing

ISBN 978-1-84928-383-0

PREFACE

Companies are continually looking for ways to better understand their performance, and identify opportunities for improvement.

Key Performance Indicators (KPIs) are measures which identify performance in achieving specific business strategies and objectives. People believe these are simple measurements that are easy to create. The mere act of measurement will cause people to change their behavior, without a lot of intervention.

Few companies realize how little value they get from their efforts to create KPIs.

Some organizations consult best practices. As best practices are designed to be applicable to a large number of companies, in many different environments, they often identify only the most common KPIs; the ones easiest to measure. Using only best practice recommendations, without adapting them to your particular environment, leaves you at risk of developing inappropriate measures, misinterpreting alerts, or taking the wrong road to remediation. KPIs are contextual and unique to each organization. One size does not fit all, and definitely not over time. You need to get down to the operational level to succeed.

Implementing a KPI process is all about changing behavior. The words in the phrase, *People – Process – Tools*, are in that order for a reason. If People don't embrace the activity, then the Process and Tools won't matter. Changing people's behavior is one of the hardest things we do in business, and something IT people find most difficult.

This is one in a series of books designed to help you understand, at an operational level, how to implement new processes, and make the necessary changes to people's behavior. This volume shows you how others have implemented effective KPI management systems in a business environment similar to that you face every day. It is a practical look at what worked, what failed, and the traps to avoid at the operational level.

Learn from their lessons and avoid their mistakes.

ABOUT THE AUTHOR

Mr McLean is a consultant who has designed, implemented and operated processes supporting ITSM for over 10 years. He has worked in IT for over 20 years. He was a peer reviewer during development of the OGC ITIL®[1] v3 Service Strategy Best Practice. He has developed and delivered ITSM courseware customized to company-specific operational practices and needs. He has worked in the US and the Middle East.

Mr McLean is the author of *The ITSM Iron Triangle: Incidents, Changes and Problems*, and *No One of Us Is As Strong As All of Us: Services, Catalogs and Portfolios*.

Mr McLean's consultancy focuses on fusing best practices from multiple ITSM relevant standards, into practical operational processes optimized for each organization's particular environment and needs. He provides this support at the design, implementation and daily operation levels.

Among other honors, Mr McLean holds an ITIL Manager's Certificate in IT Service Management, an ISO20000 Consultant Manager Certificate, and an ISO20000 Professional: Management and Improvement of ITSM Processes Certificate.

Mr McLean holds both Bachelor's and Master's degrees from Cornell University.

Mr McLean resides in Chicago, Illinois, US.

---

[1] ITIL® is a Registered Trade Mark of the Cabinet Office.

ACKNOWLEDGEMENTS

I wish to thank the following people, without whom none of this would have been possible.

My clients, users, and customers, for allowing me to learn and improve by serving them.

My managers and leaders, for trusting me with opportunities that made me grow.

My peers, for challenging my habits and making me continually assess and improve my deliverables.

My manuscript reviewers: Dave Jones, Pink Elephant and H.L. (Maarten) Souw RE, Enterprise Risk and QA Manager, UWV, for their insightful and constructive guidance.

My editors, proofreaders, publishing, marketing and other associates at IT Governance Publishing, for their patience and tireless support, especially Vicki Utting, the Publishing Production Manager.

My teachers and mentors, for their tolerance of my ignorance, persistence in their instruction, and patience with my endless questions.

My employees, students and mentees, for allowing me to grow by helping them learn.

My family, for tolerating my single-minded focus.

And my wife, Patricia, for being my rock and constant companion.

CONTENTS

INTRODUCTION

IT organizations love measurement. People in IT have a quantitative mindset, and are comfortable comparing things on a numerical basis. Most can rattle off a long series of what they believe to be Key Performance Indicators (KPIs). They see KPIs as simple calculations best left to machines, or preconfigured in vendor tool sets.

Unfortunately, developing KPIs that meet the needs of IT and our business partners, is more complicated than that. It doesn't have to be hard or arcane, however, it does need to be thoughtful. It needs integrated goals, meaningful measures, data with integrity, and specialized reporting that examines essential outcomes rather than milestones.

This narrative story provides a collection of lessons from real-world experiences in building these critical processes, while overcoming the challenge of changing people's behavior to support them.

You may have already met some of the characters in the book.

Do you know leaders whose support for you constantly vacillates? Ever had peers who only support you if it stymies their rivals? What about people who are deceptive and distort critical data, based on goals unrelated to yours?

These are some of the behavior challenges best practices don't address, yet you must overcome in order to succeed.

Please remember this story, while based on actual events, has been fictionalized. All persons, places, organizations and events appearing in this work are fictitious. Any resemblance to real people, living or dead, is entirely coincidental. Any resemblance to actual places, organizations or events, is entirely coincidental.

CHAPTER 1: SO EASY EVEN A CHILD COULD DO IT

I sat quietly in our CIO's office, trying to adopt the appearance of being present, yet still not eavesdropping – and it wasn't easy. Across the desk, Jessica, the CIO, carried on a phone conversation unrelated to our meeting. At least I hoped it was unrelated. Based on the side of the conversation I couldn't ignore, it was not one where you wanted to be the subject of the discussion.

It was striking how plain and functional her office appeared. With its standard size and furniture, it displayed that corporate neutral, impersonal space guaranteed to offend no one. Yet by comparison to those belonging to other senior leaders, it was positively austere. Although Lee, my last manager, had reported to her, he'd filled his much larger office with personality, decorated with antiques and special order equipment that were all designed to demonstrate he was special and superior.

I was glad that Lee had been shipped back out to the field. He was a self-centered jerk, whose parting gift had been to tag me with a phony, bad performance review, and force me onto a 90-day performance improvement plan (PIP). Being on a PIP meant that if you didn't remedy the deficiencies laid out within 90 days, you would be summarily dismissed, and left with bad references regarding your time at the company.

Lee had done it just to demonstrate to me, and anyone watching, that he was powerful and in charge. It didn't matter to him that he'd left me in a situation where if I made one tiny mistake at any time in the next three months,

I would be out the door and struggling again to find a decent job in a lousy economy. The only thing Lee ever cared about was himself and his own advancement. The idea of teamwork – that No One of Us Is As Strong As All of Us, was totally foreign to him. The fact that he'd been promoted because of all I had accomplished, made me even angrier.

Regardless that the PIP was unjustified, human resources, HR, had been a willing co-conspirator with Lee. Employees sometimes make the mistake of thinking HR is on their side in conflicts with management. They forget that it is called "human resources" because it is about helping leaders maximize the benefits of the company's investment in people. Those in HR were mostly good people stuck doing the job management defined for them.

"I don't care about that," said Jessica to the person on the phone. She shook her head from side to side. With a note of frustration in her voice, she said, "Look, I'm not trying to be cruel or punitive, but it is wrong for us to drag this out. If someone is not able to do the work required for their role, and we have no other roles available for them, then it is time for us to part ways. It's not fair to their peers who have to fill in for them; to our organization who needs that skill set; or to the company and stockholders who are not getting fair value for what they are paying."

Jessica silently nodded up and down a few times before interjecting. "Yes, I know that, Helmut. But it is part of your role to help us deal with this, without disrupting the flow of business."

So she was having someone fired. Helmut was the VP of Human Resources, and always played a role in these actions in IT. He made sure it was all done legal and proper, so there would be little risk of lawsuits, or other unfortunate incidents. I hoped she wasn't pulling a "Lee," and doing it to demonstrate her power. There was no question that with a single word she could have me out the door, carrying a box with my personal possessions.

"Look, Helmut," said Jessica. "I honor the many years of service they gave to the company, and am grateful for all the times they went above and beyond to deliver results. And yes, I remember personally giving them an award for an outstanding contribution. But that was two years ago. You understand as well as I that we cannot afford to carry people based solely on what they did in the past. It's nothing personal. This is a business."

There were a few moments of silence before Jessica said, "Good. Then we're aligned on this. So you will handle it such that it gets done by close of business today, yes? A quick, clean break is best for all. The sooner they get on with the next phase of their life, the better." She nodded once more. "That's great. No, don't bother calling. I don't need to speak with them when they go. Just text me before you do it, so I can make sure the appropriate members of my staff are aware. Let me know if you plan to send out a communication about it, and if you need any messaging from me."

Jessica hung up the phone. "Sorry about the interruption, Chris, but the timing dictated I take that call. It was an important HR matter. Can I count on your discretion and confidentiality regarding the matters discussed"?

I nodded. "Actually, I wasn't paying attention, so I'm not even sure what was said. I was thinking through some things I need to finish this afternoon. I'm focused on my work."

Jessica smiled. "Good. Now back to where we were before the interruption. As I was starting to say, I'm concerned that ever since Lee, your manager, was promoted out to the field, it left you without day-to-day management support while you are under a performance improvement plan deadline. I've been worried you might lose your way, and not be able to recover. Under these conditions, even a single misstep could result in a permanent separation that I suspect you do not want. Unfortunately, we've been reorganizing IT, and the shortage of managers means there is no one for you to report to other than me at the moment."

Jessica shifted in her chair and leaned across the desk, "Frankly, I don't have the time to give you the support you really need ..."

Jessica paused and looked at me silently. It only took an instant to realize what she was waiting for. It is never good form to imply your CIO is slacking off, regardless of whether or not it was true. C-level executives have egos too. Theirs are just bigger and hungrier than the average persons.

I sat up straight, and said what I knew was the mandatory response, "You are selling yourself short, Jessica. I know you'll do everything you can to help me change to meet the goals of my performance improvement plan, subject to your other more critical responsibilities. I understand the work is on my shoulders, not yours."

I tried hard not to choke as I said the words. I didn't believe any of them, but I had learned early in my tenure at the company that sometimes the truth is situational.

"Jessica, you've always been much more generous with your time than you give yourself credit. I won't need to meet with you about everything. I can learn how to improve simply by modeling my behavior after yours, and the other employees around me. If I needed someone to walk me through every step of my job every day, I'd clearly be unable to do the work required for my role, so it would be time for us to part ways."

It wasn't until the words were already out that I realized I'd recited, virtually, a direct quote of what Jessica had said to describe the person she wanted fired; the phone conversation that I wasn't supposed to be listening in on. Jessica had seemed to be willing to give me a chance to succeed, or at least not try to get me fired as Lee did. Had my unthinking word choice just changed all that, so now she'd think I was making fun of her? There seemed no way to recover.

All I could do was to change the subject and keep talking. "When do you think I will have a new manager ... someone at a level closer to mine, so that I will be less of a distraction to you and your work"?

Jessica grinned. "I think we are close to identifying a solution to this situation, but it would be inappropriate for me to say anything until everything is finalized. You'll just have to wait in suspense like everyone else."

"That's fine. I'm confident you'll tell me what I need to know, when I need to know it." I hoped my nod of compliance with comfortable ignorance might help bury the earlier faux pas.

Jessica pulled a sheaf of papers from a folder on her desk. "To help you through your performance improvement plan, I've come up with a project that will allow you to make an awesome first impression on our leadership team. It's

7

something that will help you get off to a great start, and at the same time demonstrate some of the behaviors the PIP identified as missing."

She slid a few slick, glossy product brochures across the table to me. "This is a new application the company purchased earlier this year. It uses all the ITSM best practices to provide an integrated service management capability. It handles our service management needs, from incident management to continual improvement. It's called the service management tool, or SMT for short."

I nodded. "I didn't know it was fully rolled out and ready for production."

"It was quietly launched a few months ago. Nothing formal yet. Data is being collected and utilized. Key groups have already had awareness and task training. Additional training will begin for IT at large in a couple of weeks. Information was highly controlled by the SMT team, to avoid distractions to the rest of the organization. After all, we wouldn't want to start a major communication program across the entire company and then not be able to deliver. I've always found it is best to manage the communications tightly. That way your performance and your commitments are always aligned. Think of that as a lesson for your PIP."

I glanced through the sales brochures. "The SMT looks very cool. I'm looking forward to getting a chance to see it in action."

"Not as much as I am," said Jessica. "This is a huge financial commitment for the company, but I think it will quickly pay off." Jessica reached across the table and took a brochure. She thumbed through it to a particular page, and handed it back, while pointing at one section on the page.

"Personally, I'm excited to finally get this. It should make my job a lot easier and respond to the requests I keep getting from the CEO."

She pointed to a section titled, "Key Performance Indicators – Metrics of Significance."

"Key Performance Indicators, KPIs, are really hot right now," she said. "Everyone, from the Board of Directors on down, is looking for them. With the struggling economy, we need to measure all of our activities, so we can figure out if we're going in the right direction. There is no room for missteps. One of the great things about the SMT tool is that it natively produces several hundred of them, without any customization on our part."

"That's great. You said something about an impressive project. Is it connected to this"?

"Actually, yes. Not only will it be a critical piece of management information out of the system, it will also help your new boss baseline the performance for each area in IT. That's important, because one of his or her new responsibilities will be to maintain a watch over what we are doing through these measures."

I was nervous at the idea of setting a baseline for my new boss, much less for everyone else. What if it was wrong, and made things look better than they really were, so any improvement he had would have to overcome that. "Okay, so what does it involve"?

"Your work will be to conduct an assessment of the first use of the tool to provide these metrics. We've rolled it out for the service desk and desktop support. I want you to assess the tool's effectiveness in terms of KPIs, for the performance in one of these areas, and make suggestions for further adjustments. How you do it is up to you as the project owner."

Now I was confused. What was my project? Was it to get SMT rolled out, or did it have something to do with those KPIs, or was it something else? Jessica was being really vague, but there was no way I was going to tell her I didn't understand, and look stupid. That would be a great way for someone on a PIP to get fired immediately. Fortunately, Jessica was on a roll.

"In the interest of helping you successfully complete your PIP, I've kept the focus narrow." Jessica began sketching on a blank sheet of paper. "Use what we've done in the service desk area, or the desktop support, as a template for ways we can roll out further KPI programs across the rest of IT. Once people see what the tool does, everyone will want to become an early adopter."

"Start small and grow big by word of mouth. That makes sense to me."

Jessica began collecting the SMT documents and putting them in the folder on her desk.

"In the interest of helping you succeed in your PIP, I recommend you collect the relevant metrics from the SMT tool, and then verify these are the right measures. That will point out the gaps you need to plug. Since they are both accustomed to measurements, they should be quick and easy adopters of the new measures. But it is your assignment. I'm merely specifying the 'what.' The 'who' and the 'how' is up to you."

I was no fool. I wasn't going to pick some other group after she had suggested those two. Doing that would be like telling her she didn't know what she was doing.

1: So Easy Even a Child Could Do It

"I think the service desk is the best place to start," I said. "I worked with Manny when I was doing that project for Lee on defining services. We seemed to get along quite well."

"Manuel Sanchez"? asked Jessica. "You must have missed the messaging. Mr Sanchez left the company two weeks ago, to pursue greater success elsewhere. I'm sure Helmut could get you a copy of the communication."

I shook my head. "That's not necessary. Who is his replacement"?

"Temporarily, we have a consultant named Molly, who has taken responsibility for the service desk. She has quite a bit of experience, and we all hold high hopes for her success."

"Then I guess I should go find Molly and get this underway."

So Manny had been fired. I wondered for a moment what rule he had broken, or which leader he had offended, or if they had simply got rid of him for no good reason at all, much as Lee had tried to do with me.

"Wonderful," said Jessica. "This assignment is so easy even a child could do it. However, it's your attitude that's important here. I hope you appreciate that we put you on a PIP because we care about you and your success. I'd like you to be able to stay with us. It would be a shame if we had to let you go."

There was a threat reminder in there. It had been expertly delivered ... an iron fist inside a soft, velvet glove.

"There will be a meeting of my directs tomorrow, and I'd like you to go through the SMT material, and provide my staff with an overview of how you would measure the service desk, and what KPIs would be important for us to track. Just use your best judgment of what the service desk should be tracking to manage itself for now. We can always change it later."

As I walked out of Jessica's office, her last words still rung in my head. I couldn't recall the last time something had been done here, and then was changed once leadership had seen it. No one who said things weren't cast in stone had ever worked here before.

Tips that would have helped Chris

Choose outcomes and impacts over actions and efforts

KPIs are about measuring outcomes and impacts which are usually ongoing and repeating. Project plans are about measuring actions and efforts which typically are events and tasks. KPIs, metrics and measures are all different kinds of information. They are not the same. All KPIs are metrics, but not all metrics are KPIs.

Ensure clarity

It is essential when working on ITSM implementations, or any other kind of assignment, that there is absolute clarity about what constitutes "done," and how success is measured. In the absence of clarity, people will make up their own definitions, and mismatched expectations will be the result. There is no harm in asking for clarification. Sometimes asking for clarification will actually help the leader see a gap they hadn't considered. There are no stupid questions, only unasked ones.

Own the expectations

People have high, often unrealistic expectations, in terms of content, quality, and time to deliver for what they see as simple projects. The further they are from the details of what has to happen, the more unrealistic their assumptions will be. Don't be afraid to reset expectations, or at least hold them in abeyance until you have had a chance to examine the situation. People may not like that, but it is essential you remain in control of expectations. If you don't set the expectations, they will, and usually to your detriment.

CHAPTER 2: I'D THOUGHT THINGS WERE GOING RATHER WELL

I slapped the side of the terminal as the screen went dark, and all the data I'd loaded into the SMT for the last 30 minutes dissipated into the ether. "Your mother was a toaster and your father was a cockroach who loved her because she'd never been cleaned," I snapped.

I'd yelled loud enough for anyone on our floor to hear; if there had been anyone else near my cube at 1.30 am. While everyone else was gone, either sleeping or partying, I was stuck here trying to get this stupid SMT tool to work well enough for me to get the data I needed for my presentation tomorrow morning. The fact that I was crunching at the last minute was not my fault. I had relied on our CIO's opinion of how easy it was to use.

Apparently, while the vendor's consultants had gotten the software running, they hadn't yet been able to get it properly tuned. They euphemistically referred to it as, "Post implementation testing using real-time incremental input and removal validation." As long as the check cleared, they were happy. Months ago they promised it would be fixed real soon. I just kept telling myself this was what our leadership called progress.

After all my struggles, Jessica's comment that this was going to be so easy a child could do it, was clear proof that she had no idea the work involved beyond what was in the glossy sales brochure.

I had been wrong to pay attention to anything my leaders said that required operational understanding and experience, simply because it had been 20 years since any of them had to deliver any tactical work. Their world was now nothing more than making decisions based on proposals fed to them by their minions, and occasionally giving out assignments.

To any objective observer, the fact that her advice to me was totally wrong, should be all the proof needed that any delays or errors were not my fault, and should not count against my PIP. Unfortunately, even though I'd been working here a few months, I couldn't remember anyone who was a truly objective observer.

While the system rebooted, I scrawled a large, "Save Your Work" sign on the back of a yellow sticky note, and attached it just above my screen. As soon as SMT finished loading, I began keying in the data as fast as I could. The system was slow and cranky. As near as I could tell, the vendor had bought a bunch of old mainframe tools from a series of failing companies, and then bundled them together under a common interface for a client-server environment. It was somewhat like building an automobile by taking the parts of a dozen 20 year old wrecks, and shoving them into a modern chassis. The only thing it seemed to do reliably, was lose input data, and nothing in their help information was even remotely useful, beyond the admonition to frequently save my work.

It was bad enough this hodge-podge of a system was so slow it took three hours to load what should have taken 30 minutes, but the fact that my presentation was barely eight hours away moved this from frustrating to emergency. Fortunately, if the documentation I had read on the system was correct, it would automatically produce an enormous list of service desk metrics that were perfect for every occasion, and that was great news. Perhaps Jessica had been right about that portion of it. Once I got the data loaded, everything should be easy enough for a child to do.

My first quick look through the documentation had shown some good KPIs that any senior leader would want to know about the service desk. There were things like, length of call, time to resolve, dropped calls, wait times, and more. Once I had the data loaded, my only concern would be whether to use them all, or cherry-pick the most impressive ones. This is where my psychology came in.

I was going to delegate upward, and let Jessica's staff decide what KPIs I should have the service desk produce. I figured there was no way I could pick the right set to satisfy everyone, no matter how good my judgment was. So the answer was obvious. I'd give them all the KPIs the system could produce for the service desk, and let them read through to decide what they wanted. As a bonus, it meant I didn't need to do much more after I got the data loaded, other than logically organize them.

Hopefully my new manager's peers would tell him about what a great piece of work I'd produced. Leaders like to demonstrate their value by making little changes, just to show how their higher perspective is invaluable. I snickered when the image of my pet dog marking his territory came into my head. While I was in such a promising frame of mind, I also promised to keep my desk clean … to get more sleep … to help other people. The list went on and on, just like the data.

I worked till dawn and then some. By meeting time I was tired to the point of being seriously cranky. Fortunately, that only lasted until I got to the conference room. It was nearly a full house; and like an old racehorse returning to the track, being there gave me the strength to jump into it. Every chair at the table in the conference room was occupied. Even some of the broken chairs at the back had people perched nervously on them. I guess when the CIO invites you to a meeting, you show up, no matter how important you think you are.

I was a little irritated because there were people at the meeting who definitely had not been on the invite list. I always thought it strange how an invitation to a meeting was construed to give you a license to bring along anyone else you wanted, without getting an approval from the organizer. I knew most of the uninvited guests. Some were the worker bees for the actual invitees, so I guess that made sense. That way the invitees wouldn't have to bother explaining what needed to be done, or why. It also meant they could work on other things, and not really pay attention, since their underlings were there to take notes and ask questions. There were some suits in the back that I had never seen before. I figured they were just visitors from corporate. No one in IT wore a suit. Or maybe they were people like Lee, in from the field, because they had a much more formal dress code than we did.

10 minutes into the presentation, I was getting head nods, note taking, and all the positive signs that it was going really well. Even some of the leaders stopped texting and were actually paying attention. At least it seemed that way, right up to the point where one of the suits in the back stopped me mid-sentence and said, "I am concerned that some individuals might interpret this information as a suggestion we use all of the measures you've listed over the last two slides. I'm not sure how many there are, but it looks like there are quite a few. I would greatly appreciate it if you would clarify for the group which of them you

would like to recommend the service desk should adopt or modify."

The conference room went silent. Everyone in the room stopped what they were doing and stared at me. This had to be someone ignorant of how KPIs work, and unfamiliar with the norms for meetings here. I had never interrupted someone during their presentation to ask what they meant, and I didn't think it right they should treat me differently.

I shot a furtive glance at Jessica. I couldn't judge her expression or body language, but I wasn't picking up a happy vibe in the room.

I turned toward the suit, and in an effort to buy some time to consider the most appropriate answer, said, "Excuse me? You have some concerns about the material we've been discussing"? Repeating unanticipated questions back to people in the guise of clarification, was always a great way to buy a few more seconds to think through an answer.

The suit stood up in a precise, formal and almost mechanical way. He was a tall man with black hair and a swarthy complexion. In a resonant voice, with a noticeable east European accent, he said, "I merely note that you are proposing the use of a large number of measures to manage and evaluate the service desk. Unless the service desk manager has a background or experience with metric design or management by metric, they may find all of that information overwhelming and counterproductive. How did they react when you proposed so many measures to them"?

He paused for a moment, letting his words sink in. His facial expression was neutral, almost as if he were simply a puppet who didn't care and someone had given him the question to ask, even though he didn't understand it.

"Someone of your background and experience ... ," he continued, " ... has no trouble interpreting all of this data. I am trying to assist you by reassuring the people in the room that they should not be concerned about that because you must have some focusing slides later in your presentation that spell out exactly what you are recommending for the service desk manager and this group at large."

Two minutes ago, I had everyone in my pocket. I was proud that it was aligned with our use doctrines for SMT, as well as the overall IT policies. Now the whole pace was stumbling, and I was in danger of losing control. Whether this ignorant suit was right or wrong, I couldn't let my performance whither. I remembered one of the lessons I had learned from my last manager – whether you are right or wrong, always act confident and in charge.

I reached out and tapped on the projection screen beside me.

On the screen was displayed a grid that contained part of the list of Key Performance Indicators (KPIs) that came with the SMT tool, this included their purpose and frequency of measure. Actually, I had cut and pasted the grid directly out of the SMT manual, but since I was offering all of them to the group, and there was no chance they would ever read the SMT manual, I'd figured it was the most expeditious course. Besides, it was this very same leadership body that had decreed there was to be no customization of the SMT tool. Only configuration changes would be considered. I knew from my own personal experience that was something they got absolutely right. The last place I'd worked had spent years customizing their system, to the point where it couldn't be upgraded, and every time they added one thing, it broke three others.

These were KPIs that no one could argue about. They'd been developed by the experts who'd created the SMT tool. These KPIs were based on years' of experience and current, best practice. These measures were as close to expert selections as you could get. If you couldn't understand or manage your group using these KPIs, then you shouldn't be managing anything. An executive might not see that right away, but that was why I was here. Although I didn't know much about these KPIs, I knew a lot more than they did, and in the land of the ignorant, even the tiniest bits of knowledge made you king. My job was simply to explain why these were the right KPIs, and ensure they were made available to leadership. With the brainpower of the SMT experts behind me, this was so easy even a child could do it.

You couldn't run a service desk without these measures. The first half-dozen included, inbound contacts per agent per month, outbound contacts per agent per month, percentage of calls answered in 30 seconds, call abandonment rate, and average minutes of handle time. I was confident these were good things to measure.

As part of its feature set, the SMT tools printed out mini-charts, showing values for these measures over the last few months, as well as a corresponding stoplight, giving an overall red, yellow or green status of the metric. They were segmented into three areas; customer, financial and operations. Each of the three areas was further divided into a number of sections, and each section was further broken out into multiple, specific sub-metrics. There were 127 sub-metrics. It may have been a pain to load the data, but once it was in there, the KPIs sliced and diced the information in every way you could possibly want.

Given the number of measures, I had to print it in a very small font that was a little hard to read, but that wasn't the point. This was everything that mattered top to bottom and front to back. These reports had all the data anyone would need to make any important decision. They had to. They were the reports the SMT builders had determined were the most important ones to have. That made it the perfect executive dashboard for our service desk. With those 127 metrics, an executive could rule the world ... or at least the service desk.

I'd given each attendee a spreadsheet with all of the same information on it, so they could read along. I'd had to shrink it down, so it would fit on standard-sized paper, but that was okay. These were leaders. They weren't going to actually do anything with this beyond pass it on to their teams. They just needed to be impressed with all the data being presented.

That's something I'd finally realized last night. The real purpose of my assignment, and this meeting, was to introduce how the SMT tool would be the new executive scorecard, and that leadership had made the right decision by purchasing the SMT tool, especially since it was the cheapest alternative the company had considered. Leadership had saved the company a lot of money by going with the lowest price solution. There was no need to spend money on tools when there were cheaper alternatives available.

Excluding the heavily scripted vendor demos, this was the first time these people had even seen the SMT tool in action, so they should have been very impressed at the value they were getting for their money, especially when they saw the cool, little red-yellow-green stoplights.

Something like that could be a real executive timesaver. At least that is where I'd thought we were going.

I reached out and poked the matrix projected onto the screen.

"The SMT tool provides the results of a series of analysis developed by experts in the field. These Key Performance Indicators, or KPIs as they are known, directly track and forecast the activities of the service desk. This provides leaders in the service desk, and at corporate, with instant real-time snapshots of service desk performance, as well as monthly historical analysis tracking the service desk's efficiency. Any variation, no matter how small, could be immediately identified in real time, and remediated before it became an issue. The objective is not to limit the number of KPIs to some arbitrary number. The price of failing to track an important KPI could be very high. The idea is to provide everyone with all of the possible data, so that no matter what concern they have, they will be able to access the information they need to make optimal decisions for the company."

The suit slowly shook his head, smiled and said, "And tell us Chris ... it is Chris, isn't it"?

I nodded.

"Tell us Chris. There are a large number of measures here. How did you decide on the selection of measures that were essential to running the business"?

"I'm not sure what you mean."

He waved his hand at the matrix on the screen, "Why did you pick these, instead of some other measures? Some of these are clearly operational and tactical, and of little use at the executive level. I think people would have much more appreciation for the work you've obviously put into this if they understood the decision logic you've developed to identify the relevant measures."

I took a deep breath. What was with this suit? Was he stupid? Wasn't he listening to what I was saying? Why was he giving me such a hard time and being such a jerk? What could he possibly care? It had to be because his boss was here and he was trying to show off ... and unfortunately, I was the means to that end. It didn't matter the subject, or even who I was. It was that disgusting phrase leadership liked to use just before they stuck the knife in, "It's not personal." That was the only thing I could think of, because he was clearly too ignorant to even understand what he didn't know. Since the rest of the audience knew even less, he could look like a genius by throwing rocks at me.

"Well, Chris ... could there be the possibility that while this is an impressive piece of work and exhaustive in its scope, that perhaps by reducing the number of metrics to a few highly focused KPIs, the decision makers could focus on the quality of the message, rather than the quantity of repeating messages? You know ... will people make better decisions if they have two meaningful and relevant KPIs, or a hundred good, but less focused metrics"?

I wasn't sure what the right approach was here.

"Thank you for your comments. You sound like you have extensive experience in this area. Do you have some KPIs in particular that you think are more valuable than the others"?

He shook his head. "I'm hardly an expert. That's for you to decide. I am merely suggesting that the number of metrics you propose may be more than decision makers can work with at once. No place I've worked before has had this many metrics. I have always been a proponent of only providing those metrics that really matter, rather than all that can be measured."

"I appreciate that, but the experts at SMT determined these are the right KPIs to have for the service desk activities, that there are neither too many, nor too few. That's why they refer to them as KPIs. To clarify terms, these are Key Performance Indicators, not metrics. I won't go into the technical detail here for this audience, but it makes a difference."

The suit nodded and was about to speak, when Jessica interrupted.

"This is a fascinating discussion that needs to be explored in more depth than we have time for in this forum. Why don't the two of you take this offline and come back to us later with a joint recommendation."

The suit smiled. "It would be my pleasure to work with Chris on this."

I nodded and bit back on my anger. The last thing you wanted to hear your work described as was fascinating. "My apologies to the group for the delay, but I'm sure you will find the rest of the material very useful when we talk again next week. In the interim, I encourage you to study the material in the presentation packages I distributed at the start of the meeting."

I could only hope that my new boss wouldn't start until after this had all blown over. This suit didn't even understand the difference between metrics and KPIs, so once I had him separated from his boss, I was confident I could roll right over him and get him thinking properly.

"I believe that is all of the material we have for today. Thank you for attending." said Jessica. People began packing up to leave. Pointing at the suit and me, Jessica said, "Will both of you please stay behind for a couple of minutes."

Good, I thought. She was probably going to chew on him for disrupting the meeting. That would make my job all the easier, not to mention personally satisfying to see someone else get yelled at for a change.

As the attendees filed out, I began packing up my materials. I wanted to get out of here as soon as Jessica was done yelling at the suit, and get back to work.

The suit sat down in a chair next to where I was working.

Jessica walked over. "I'm very sorry, Chris, but I thought I had already introduced you two. This is awkward and embarrassing because while you don't know him, he knows of you," she said.

I snapped around and looked at her, then the suit. His face was still totally unfamiliar.

"Chris, I'd like you to meet Sergiu. He is your new manager. Today is his first day. In fact, this is his very first meeting here."

Sergiu stuck out his hand. I smiled and shook his hand.

My mouth said, "Welcome. It's really great to have you onboard. I'm really looking forward to working for you," while my brain screamed, "MERDE"!

Tips that would have helped Chris

Respect other people's time

It is easy to make the mistake of regurgitating everything you know when communicating to others. Remember that it took you a long time to gather all that knowledge. Asking them to process it in a matter of minutes is unrealistic, and wastes the time they spend on it. They will not appreciate having their time wasted. Focus, reduce and summarize.

Build coalitions

It is important to avoid publically presenting recommendations for action that impact the workflow or activities of others, without first obtaining their support. Work with them privately. Understand their concerns, and solicit their recommendations for the best approach to deal with the situation. They may provide you with insight you had not considered. They can even help you sell the ideas to others. It is far better to share the credit with others, than to have them challenging you at every turn.

Take it outside

Public conflict is frowned upon in almost every organization and situation. If you find that despite your best preparation you become engaged in a direct confrontation while presenting your recommendations, take the conflict offline, and resolve it privately between the two of you before continuing the presentation. It shows far more maturity and professionalism to withdraw your presentation before it is finished, than to slug it out to the end with a hostile hold-out.

CHAPTER 3: TRY TO GET IT RIGHT THIS TIME

I'd spent the last 24 hours thinking about the meeting yesterday and I still couldn't get it out of my head. I leaned back in my chair and closed my eyes, trying to get the din from the cubicles surrounding mine to drive the anger and frustration out of my head. It didn't work. I kept trying to get my thoughts focused around what had gone wrong, so I could fix it before my first official one-on-one with Sergiu – in 10 minutes.

It didn't matter what Sergiu would say. There was nothing wrong with what I'd done. The presentation was structurally sound. It was at the right level of detail for the leadership team. I'd set the right tone and expectations at the start, by telling them what this was about. It had all the features of my executive scorecard. It looked so professional, all color coded and arranged according to our company standards. I'd even reinforced the fact that we could do all of this without customization of the SMT software.

My presentation was perfect; exactly what I would want to see if I had been in the audience. The problem must have been on their end. Clearly, those leaders weren't quick enough to grasp the material, and understand what it could do for them. I chuckled, remembering that old quote about how you didn't need to be smart to be in command, just have a loud voice.

I'd been around long enough to know that if your leaders were at best ignorant, and at worst idiots, then you needed to dumb things down to their level if you wanted to succeed. The challenge was how to reconfigure it in a way that would be simple enough for them to understand. I wasn't going to let Sergiu's opinions sway me too much. I'd still make sure he thought it was his idea, and let him get the credit for it. That was going to happen no matter what. Right now, I just wanted to prove that I had been right, but it couldn't be at the cost of my job.

"Are you asleep again? People get fired for that. If you want, I can tell you a great place where no one will notice you're asleep ... or even that you're there. It's called the boardroom. The executives used to do a lot of what you're doing there, except they called it envisioning success. I guess it worked because they got themselves right out of there and into a nice, plush headquarters."

I immediately recognized Sean's voice. He'd worked for the company almost since its beginning. His hands had built a lot of the IT core, and over time he'd worked in just about every group in IT. He was one of the few survivors from the old days. Now he was a trouble shooter for the iron triangle of IT – Incident, Change, and Problem Management. Strangely, he'd never advanced beyond the level of manager, and then only for a very brief period before asking to go back to being a worker. I never did understand that. No matter how good you were, your salary always maxed out, unless you were willing to be a manager over people. It's as if he didn't care about the money.

I'd always wondered if never moving beyond being a manager was his choice or theirs. Sean knew more about how IT worked than any two leaders I'd ever met, but was openly dismissive of people who advanced beyond the day-to-day activity. Our company had a funny view about being in management. Leadership was quite open about their belief that a management role was an honor and a privilege that everyone should aspire to achieve. In their minds, if you declined the offer to become a manager, you were clearly substandard, and your commitment to the company was questionable. For those few who took management roles and then decided to go back to operational roles, there was no alternative to leaving the company ... either under your own power, or by force. Moving into management was a one way trip.

The thing I admired most about Sean was how he always seemed to be able to get away with behaviors that would have gotten most people fired. Perhaps he had some incriminating pictures from the old days, or maybe it was his geeky sense of humor. Whatever the reason, he was one of those lucky few. For whatever reason, management seemed to cut him a lot more slack than anyone else.

Without opening my eyes, or moving, I said, "No, unlike you, I actually use my brain when I'm at work."

"Is that what you call it now? I think I prefer to call it what it is, a nap."

I sat up and swiveled the chair around. Sean was sitting opposite me in my cube. I pulled the executive dashboard material from my folio. Laying it on the table in front of him, I said, "Will you do me a favor and take a look at this? It's a presentation I gave to our management team about the new service desk dashboard we'll be providing, using the SMT tool."

Sean poked at it gently with a finger – rotating it on the table as if it were something diseased. "And they hated it, didn't they"?

"How'd you know"? I asked. "Did Sergiu send the word out already? Or worse, did Jessica"?

Sean shook his head and grinned. "Relax, no one has been spreading word of your failure ... yet. Even your new boss has been quiet about it. Try simple deductive reasoning. If it had gone well, you'd be dancing on the desk and telling everyone how great you were. You are not. You're sulking in your cube, and asking me what went wrong. Therefore you must have failed."

He picked up the thick folder, and gave an exaggerated groan to match the theatrical struggle he mimed lifting it off the table.

Fanning through the pages, he laughed and asked, "Were you planning to beat them into submission with it? That might have gotten you a better reception. Did you really expect senior leaders to wade through all this data? You've got more dials here than a jetliner. Their job is not to analyze data. Their job is to make decisions that resolve conflicts and reduce risks. They want solution proposals, not data dumps. I thought you knew that"?

"Don't be stupid," I snapped back. "That file has all the KPIs the SMT experts believe are important. Do you know how many KPIs are produced by the SMT tool? There are hundreds. I'm using the exact KPI suite for the service desk, directly as it comes from the SMT tool, but I'm summarizing them into logical groups, so they can work with a smaller set. I made it ..."

Sean cut me off mid-sentence. "Stop. Even your excuse is too long and convoluted for someone with the attention span of management. They have too many issues to balance to spend time listening to your long-winded explanations. Things need to stand on their own merit, without your presence. If they don't, then you're not preparing them right."

Sean stood up and dropped the file back on the table. It landed with a loud thud. "I'd love to help you Chris, but I made a point of staying out of this initiative. Remember, these are the people that said we could not customize any outputs from the SMT tool before they even saw what it could do, and wouldn't have to deal with it on a day-to-day basis. Even after they saw what it could do, they overruled our recommendations because they didn't have the operational experience to understand what they were asking us to do. So they bought whatever was cheapest, and met the minimum feature set as 'promised' by the vendor's salespeople." He grinned at me. "And you know how good those promises are."

Sean stood up and stopped at the entrance to my cube. "If you want to succeed, then people who have to live with this on a day-to-day basis will need to be part of the solution. Without them feeling some sense of participation and ownership in this, it will never work."

"That's why I just walked away from it," he said. "A long time ago, I learned that if you want to be in this for the long term, you've got to know when to embrace an initiative and when to run in the opposite direction. The sound you hear are my feet running in the opposite direction. If you want to figure out how to understand which KPIs you need for the service desk, you'll need Molly."

Sergiu's office was easy to find. They'd even taped up a paper name badge on the wall beside his office door. It always struck me as weird how the company would never put a replacement in the same space as the person previously in that role ... it made no sense to me.

The space for his administrative assistant was vacant. Maybe that was a new economy measure on the part of the company, or maybe he hadn't been deemed sufficiently important enough to merit that kind of support. I knocked on his open door, and then stepped through into his office.

Looking up from the papers spread all over his desk, Sergiu said, "Chris ... thank you for making time to meet with me today." He gestured to a chair in front of his desk. "Please, have a seat. Would you mind closing the door? I want our discussions, especially in light of your PIP status, to be candid and direct conversations just between us."

When your manager says they want to have a candid and direct conversation with you, it is never good. The only thing worse is if they add that it is also a difficult conversation. Was he planning to fire me his second day on the job?

Sergiu picked up a couple of sheets from his desk and said, "Jessica has told me that you are currently on a performance improvement plan, a PIP, for failing to meet performance expectations under your previous manager, Lee, and that she had assigned this new task to you as part of our assessment of your capabilities, and your potential to perform commensurate with your grade level and role ..." Sergiu paused for a moment, and then added, "At this company."

Sergiu put the papers back down and looked straight through me.

"All said, how would you rate your performance on this assignment so far"?

I took a deep breath and said, "KPIs are about giving people the right information they need at the right time, so they can make the best possible decisions for the company." At least that was the best I could remember of the definition in the SMT manual. Didn't matter if it was right or not, I liked the way it sounded.

"I think I delivered the right set of KPIs for the leadership team to use," I said.

Sergiu held up a copy of the thick list of KPIs I'd presented. "Did you talk to anyone else about this beforehand; get their feedback on your decisions?" He pointed at the copy. "There are a lot of measures here, and I was wondering if you decided on all of them, or if others had some voice in it? Perhaps one of the service desk managers"?

The very nature of his question implied he thought what I had done was sub-standard. Was he testing me to see if I was going to say Jessica told me to use my best judgment so I talked to no one? Somehow, the idea of blaming my CIO for what Sergiu saw as defects in my work, seemed like a bad idea.

"Thank you for the feedback," I said. "I really appreciate your guidance and insight. I was constrained by the time to deliver the presentation, and the dictate from leadership to use SMT straight out of the box. Since I wasn't allowed to make any changes to the measures, I tried to ensure I was aligned with leadership first."

"Alignment is important, but I've always found that bringing impacted people into the decision process is essential, because it gives them a feeling of ownership. People always perform better with some level of accountability. I understand I was not here to support you prior to your presentation, and I know how hard it can be to arrange for time with a CIO. However, in the future, if you ever feel there is insufficient time to prepare properly, do not hesitate to say so, and ask to reschedule. Far better to defer for a short period than to waste leadership's time with an ill-prepared presentation."

I had just been slapped, but with tremendous style. Sergiu was good ... very good. I would have to watch him carefully in the future. In his mind, I was not only producing sub-standard work, but I was wasting leadership's time. I kept a smiling face. I couldn't let him see me worry. That would only make me look less capable.

"What would you recommend as my next steps? I was planning to find Molly for starters."

Sergiu shuffled through his papers and said, "That sounds appropriate. Remember what I said about ownership and accountability. Far better to have them working with you to build a solution, than feeling like you're forcing a solution on them."

"Got it," I said. "I know you are new here, but do you know anything about what happened to Manny? I don't know if Jessica shared any additional information with you. I'd always thought he was a dependable guy. While I might not have agreed with how he ran his team, when he helped me with my work on building end-to-end services, I got to see that he always produced effective results."

Sergiu shook his head. "Sorry, I know nothing, and even if I did, that is an HR-related item which must remain confidential and on a need to know basis, to protect the privacy of the individuals involved. Be assured that whatever happened was done with the co-operation, and in the best interests, of everyone involved."

"No problem," I said. "I was just thinking about reaching out to him, just to get together some time and have a coffee or a beer."

"If you're his friend," said Sergiu. "I am sure you have his home contact information and can reach him there. Remember, Chris, change is the one constant we face, and the ability to quickly adapt is one of the most important skills we can have. That's important to completing your PIP successfully."

I gave him my best corporate smile and nodded my head. "No problem. I am good at adapting to change." Right company response on the outside, but inside I wondered how close I was to following Manny out the door.

"I'm sure you must be dealing with a lot of change, coming on board in the midst of all this," I said. "If there is anything I can do to support your transition, please ask." A little flattery for my new boss couldn't hurt, especially for someone on a PIP.

Sergiu shuffled through some more documents and gestured toward the door. "Thank you for your offer. However, if I were you, I would focus on my PIP. That means you'll need to find Molly. I'd start over in the service desk building."

Tips that would have helped Chris

Don't let your pride hobble you

You will make mistakes. You will offend people. You will say the wrong thing at the worst possible time. You will do things you'll wish you could retract later. It happens to everyone. Owning up to your mistakes, expressing contrition and a willingness to remediate them, will go a long way to restoring your image in the minds of those around you.

See your work through the eyes of others

There will be times when you produce work that is not effective in the eyes of others. Sometimes this is due to poor communication on your part. Communication takes place in the mind of the recipient, regardless of what was intended. Sometimes it is due to the work not being good enough, but you haven't looked at the work with a critical enough eye. You become too attached to the work and forget that it is only lines on paper. Try to step back and look at the work as someone without your knowledge and experience would. Put yourself in their place.

CHAPTER 4: THE TRIVIAL MANY VERSUS THE MEANINGFUL FEW

I had no experience with Molly. The word was that her work was high quality. Whether or not it was good value for the company, or necessary, was another issue decided way above my pay grade. Molly wasn't an employee. She was one of the SMT consultants who had descended on the company before the ink was dry on the sales contract. That was over two years ago, and they were still here. I'd heard that their contract had just been extended, and that they would probably be here for at least another six months, helping us get the tool working properly. There was even a rumor they were looking to expand the scope of their contract beyond just making the tool operational.

That was something I never quite understood. I knew tools like SMT were a complex piece of software and all, but how could something that was supposed to help us, take over two years of effort by the developer's experts to set up and get running? It always gave me the gnawing feeling we were paying more to make the tool operational than we paid to purchase it in the first place. It also seemed that we had to dedicate an equal number of our company's staff to work with them, so there were no savings there.

The whole set-up was something the executive team had agreed to when they signed the contract. I assumed they knew what they were doing, and had access to facts that the rest of us did not. Still, it seemed to me that even for a complex piece of enterprise software, if it was that difficult to install, was it ever going to be useful, or even worth it? At least the software was cheap compared to the alternatives, so there was some benefit to the company in that.

SMT seemed to have three types of consultants. There were some whose job was just to interact with the client, and make them feel good and smart for buying the software from the vendor. They seemed to alternate between saying, "I'm sorry," and "The invoice is overdue." Then there were the super-brilliant geeks, whose role was to interact with the application, but never with any customers. They were the ones with no social skills and no internal filters ... the ones who could lose the account in a moment, but were essential to making it all work. They had that annoying tendency to tell clients things that are inappropriate, simply because they are true. They were rarely allowed around any customer employees without a handler, who could make sure no permanent damage was done.

It appeared that Molly was one of the third kind ... fill-ins. These were people who could be dropped into specific roles that were necessary to make the tool work, but either not being done at the company, or else being done so poorly that the person in that role needed to be replaced for the installation to succeed. Apparently, that is what had happened to Manny.

I thought it rather strange that the company would get rid of an employee, and then put a consultant from a vendor in charge of a key service management process that touched both the users and the technology teams. Regardless, it wasn't my task to evaluate that. I assumed positive intent and positive performance until shown otherwise. I'd give her the benefit of the doubt in her role.

The service desk team was housed in a two-story, non-descript building that looked like thousands of other modern office-park boxes. It was built to maximize internal space and minimize cost. Externally, there were no signs it was a part of the company. The only clue it was even occupied was the full parking lot.

Despite my company ID pass, I still had to sign in as a guest at reception, and wait for an escort. No one got near the service desk without special approval.

It was the job of the service desk to process calls. Anything that took them away from that was bad. Their mission was to serve the customer. They were a production shop, just like a manufacturing line, and any distraction could cost the company real money.

A few minutes after I'd signed in with security and added the guest badge to my shirt, the locked door behind the front desk guard opened, and out bounded a woman who just seemed to beam energy into the room.

"Hi," she blurted out with a big smile. "You must be Chris. I'm Molly and I'm so glad you are here. Are you ready"?

It was uncanny. Just having Molly in the room for a few minutes made me want to get up and do things. There was something almost contagious about her attitude and energy. I could see why leadership liked her.

I nodded. She turned and quickly walked back through the door. "Let's go."

Within a few moments, we were walking along the edge of the enormous cube farm which contained the spaces for the workers of the service desk. It was much as I remembered, and a place I'd never want to work.

Modern building techniques had allowed construction of the space with no internal pillars blocking the view. The small cubes were barely big enough for a desk, chair and cabinet. These were low-wall cubes, without even a pretense of privacy. Walls were just four feet high; slightly concealing the sitting occupants from their neighbors. Most were occupied by people wearing headsets, and all talking at once.

On the far side, an enormous monitor was visible from every cube. It gave real-time updates, in charts, of the number of calls in queue, abandoned call rates, average call time, and a number of other key performance indicators for the day, the week and the month. Other monitors provided muted weather and news events, with closed caption streams crawling along the bottom of the images.

While I found the din from the multitude of simultaneous conversations stifling, and almost overwhelming, Molly seemed to feed on it, almost as if it recharged her energy, and wound her up even more than before.

Molly made a point of stopping at several of the cubes where people were working. She didn't stop their conversations. She simply popped in, grinned that enormous energetic smile of hers, and gave them silent applause. On some, she dropped little gold colored cards, about the size of a business card. When she saw I was trying to see what was on them, she handed one to me, as we continued toward her office. It had the words, "You've Been Recognized! 25 Way2Go Points."

I was grateful for the quiet when we stepped inside Molly's heavily soundproofed office, and she closed the door. To her left, the wall was glass, providing an unrestricted view of the nodding heads and flashing screens. Directly opposite her desk was a wall of monitors that seemed to replicate everything that was being shown to the service desk workers on the floor. Behind her desk was a console with headset, that allowed her to listen in on any conversation being conducted by the team. On her desk was a stack of unsigned birthday and anniversary cards.

I handed the gold card back to her and asked, "Motivation by recognition"?

Molly nodded. "Feedback on performance comes in all kinds of ways. It's not just numbers. People need feedback when they are doing things well, not just when they make mistakes. Getting points opens you up to a whole set of rewards that you can select based on your preference. IT is notorious for giving people negative feedback when they make mistakes. What too many IT leaders don't understand, is that people thrive and do their best only when they get positive feedback for what they are doing right. Using the stick will cause people to do just enough, not to get beaten or fired. Using the carrot will cause people to consistently excel. So I offer people who do the right things, incentives that are not available to others."

"Doesn't that open us up to potential legal suits based on fairness"? I knew the company was quite paranoid about anything that added the risk of legal action, no matter how frivolous.

"Only if you don't document why you handed out the points. If I take some heat for recognizing people doing a special job, I'll accept that any day. From a leadership standpoint, the rewards people get are secondary to the act of seeing people around them being recognized. That's the motivator and the affirmation. If you work hard, you will be recognized. That's a whole lot more effective than a seven point improvement in a numerical measure."

She pointed to the chair opposite her desk. "Would you rather sit or stand"?

I smiled. That was not a question I'd heard at this company before. Although after seeing Molly in action, it felt right in character. The only thing that surprised me at the moment was I'd expected her office to be littered with empty, energy drink containers.

"I'll sit," I said. "I have some information I'd like to show you."

She seemed slightly disappointed, as she dropped down into her chair. It seemed an almost unnatural place for her.

I pointed to the stack of unsigned cards on her desk. "You must have a lot of friends and family."

She giggled, and pointed to the service desk workers out on the floor. "They're part of my friends and family. I depend on them every day. If they don't succeed, I fail. The least I can do is send them a personal note on their birthday and their hiring anniversary, letting them know how much I appreciate all they give up to be here, and how important they are to the company and each of us associated with it."

Molly certainly was different from the managers I'd seen here before. She was definitely not the kind of person the company hired. She was a disruptor. The hiring here was more conservative. They hired people they thought would be safe for the existing organization. People who wanted to change things might push them into unfamiliar territory, and that meant uncertainty, and uncertainty meant risk, and they would do anything to avoid risk. No one ever got fired for not taking risks, but taking them often led to getting fired.

"So how may I serve you"? she asked.

As I pulled the KPI presentation material from my case and slid it across the desktop to her, part of me wondered if she was just leading me on with her positive front ... that it was all part of an elaborate ruse, designed to make me let down my guard, before she took advantage of the situation. Could I trust her not to use my disclosures against me ... to use the knowledge to advance her own situation at my expense? That's what everyone had seemed to do before. That's how I'd ended up on this PIP. The test would come when I told her I was assigned to put measures in place to evaluate how her area worked.

I took a deep breath, smiled, and said, "I've been tasked with establishing recommendations for leadership metrics across the company using the SMT tool. That includes the service desk. I was told you had an instinctive handle on this area, and with the change in leadership here, it seemed like an opportune time to establish an appropriate baseline."

Molly quickly fanned through the deck.

"This is an incredible amount of work," she said. "I can tell you put a lot of thought and energy into it, and that you really know your subject matter. Would you like some suggestions on how to make it even better, from someone who is less familiar with the tool than you are"?

I nodded.

"Please be understanding with me in my ignorance. You may have already considered some of these suggestions, and discarded them for good reason."

I shook my head. "Molly, there are no bad ideas, even if they've been heard before. I'm sure I will benefit from anything you have to say."

Listening to myself talk, I felt like I had picked up whatever it was that Molly had. Although I appreciated Molly's high energy and positive attitude toward her co-workers, I felt like it created a layer between me and the direct feedback I wanted. I wasn't a child. All I wanted was the straight story. I needed to know what was wrong, not have someone drown me in kindness. If I didn't like the answer, then so be it. Give me the straight truth and let's move on.

Molly smiled and said, "Thanks. There is so much here that the average person just can't absorb it all. Even if they could, who has the patience for that much detail"?

Sergiu had implied that in the presentation, but I still wasn't convinced. "So you think I should ask people to make decisions on incomplete information? What if they look at the wrong KPIs and make a bad decision"?

Molly shook her head. "Too much information is worse than not enough. It gives people the false perception they are being more precise, when actually many of the metrics they use duplicate each other, so they end up overweighting some areas, and underweighting others in their decision-making process."

"That makes no sense at all," I said. "Look at your predecessor, Manuel. He had dozens of KPIs to measure the performance of his team. What are you suggesting, that you only use one or two KPIs"?

Molly nodded. "Yes, look at your predecessor and where he is." She paused for a moment, as if to make sure I got the point. "Not all metrics are KPIs, and what may be a KPI for me, is not necessarily a KPI for leadership. Metrics all come with points of view, and what is a key measure for me to run my organization, may not be a key measure for leadership to run the company."

"Even if I agree that somehow less is more," I said, "How can I know which ones are the right ones? I'd have to know more about every operation in the company, and every SMT measure, than anyone else. That's impossible. We can't customize the SMT tool, and there are no qualitative measures available from the SMT tool. You of all people should know that."

"Do all your measures have to come from the SMT tool? What about things that don't lend themselves to quantitative event based measurements? Don't they matter too"?

I stopped cold. She had a good point. I hadn't even considered things outside the scope of the tool.

Molly must have understood the look of confusion on my face.

"While I am concerned with the effectiveness of my teams in meeting the needs of our customers, I am also concerned about the efficiency with which they do it. So I have some KPIs associated with that. Those are measures that, while interesting to leadership, are not true decision-making KPIs for them."

She stood up in front of the white board, and drew a picture of two boxes with a double-headed arrow between them. One box was labeled "Service Desk – Inside Out," and the other labeled "Customer – Outside In."

"I'm very concerned with the measures that evaluate performance from the inside out ... measures that look at how well I operate, as observed from inside my organization. Those are my KPIs. I'm talking about measures like, number of tickets improperly assigned; number of tickets processed by representatives over time ... things like that which tend to be very analytical and quantitative. However, leadership is more interested in how the customers perceive the experience. Those are measures like, satisfaction with the overall experience, how they were treated during the experience ... things that tend to be much more subjective and qualitative."

"Subjective experience can't produce consistent measures over time," I interrupted. "They're going to be inconsistent, and at a minimum, reflect an unconscious bias. You might just as well skip the pretense of measuring something, and just directly render your opinion."

Molly sat back down. "I know this is frustrating for someone with a quantitative engineering mindset, but not everything can be measured directly. Whether you like it or not, the ultimate measure of success in our business is how our customers feel about the service we provide. There is no analytical measure they apply. It is about as subjective as you can get. So while it's important to have quantitative measures of efficiency and effectiveness, we also need to have some measures aligned with how our customers think."

This sounded like a lot of nonsense. Up to now, I'd been really impressed with the way in which Molly was running her group. People seemed so engaged and focused, but I could see now it was just a bunch of touchy-feely stuff. Sure, you could act like that on a small scale, and hand out things like those corny cards. Wait till you had to stand up in front of a bunch of executives and tell them that you'd given out 500 recognition points this month, and sent out seven birthday cards, and then see how long you lasted. Only a consultant could think like that. They didn't care, because in a few weeks they'd be on to the next assignment. No one could act this way and keep their job over the long haul.

"So, how do you know which is which"? I asked. "Without some framework behind it, you'll have nothing more than lines on paper. The analytical effectiveness measures are clearly the most important."

"Of course you need measures aligned with how you make decisions in running your business. No one can waste company resources these days," she said. "But you also need measures that align with how your customers evaluate you, because at the end of the day, if you are not achieving customer expectations, then you are failing. It's not an either/or choice. You have to do both if you want to succeed."

I shook my head. "That's impossible. "How do I figure out which measures are the ones the customers look at? How do I get some values I can record and track? How do I set what is good, and what is bad, in the eyes of my customers, and how do I get comparison values that will be meaningful to my customers"?

Molly smiled, and after a long pause, said, "Have you ever tried asking them"?

As I sat silent, Molly's phone buzzed, and after checking the caller, she said, "I need to take this call. It's Jessica. I'm trying to get her to come and give a pep talk to my team.

Perhaps you should check with Trey, he works in the business analysis area, and spends a lot of time talking to our customers. His team does the reporting, too. Maybe he could give you some ideas. He listens to the voice of the customer."

I was almost to the door when Molly said, "Chris, you seem like you have your head in the right place, so I'm going to do something I shouldn't do. I'm going to let you know that there are going to be some changes around here shortly. There is an evaluation of how things should be done in the future going on right now, and that includes decisions about who is the right fit for the future, and who is not. If you think you're the right fit, then it is essential you figure out how to gather the voice of the customer and put it to use."

I thanked Molly, and she nodded as she began talking on the phone. I stepped out the door and into the din of the service desk call center. It was starting to become clear to me that with this new tool implementation, trying to patch up the KPI process one group at a time, made no sense at all. It was going to have to be the entire IT organization if we were to succeed.

Molly had a nice packaged speech, but that only worked if you were talking about a small contained group like hers. Trying to do something like that for the entire IT group was impossible. It was the last thing I needed messing up my KPIs. I just didn't have time to wade through a bunch of customer complaints. I had less than two weeks left to get this done, so we could better serve the customer. More importantly to me, I had a status meeting with Sergiu tomorrow morning, and absolutely no idea of how I could show him we'd made any progress.

Tips that would have helped Chris

Appreciate the style of others

You will encounter many different styles of working when enabling a major ITSM initiative. There is no right one. Some of them will seem alien, and perhaps even difficult to work with. If you are objective in examining them, you find that they are equally effective in their own way.

Use the carrot and the stick

IT is notorious for reprimanding people for failures, but not reinforcing appropriate behavior and accomplishments. Often this goes under the guise of, "That's what they are paid to do." People respond very strongly to positive gestures which reinforce an appreciation of their contribution. Consistently performing on a day-to-day basis – being dependable – is worth recognizing.

Change is hard

Don't expect people to immediately want to change their behavior the first time you ask them. People are creatures of habit, and need to understand how the change benefits everyone. Changing behavior means re-learning activities and an increased risk of stumbles. Plan to repeat your message every chance you get. Changing behavior is a long road, but can be navigated successfully, if you have determination.

CHAPTER 5: TEACHING OLD DOGS NEW TRICKS

I walked into Sergiu's office for our status meeting, right on time. That was good, because chronically late to meetings was one of the items Lee had called out on my PIP, even though I'd never been late to one while working for him. Actually, it appeared I was early, because he still had someone sitting across the desk from him. As soon as Sergiu noticed me, he stood up and motioned for me to come into his office. As he did, the new guy stood up, turned around, and extended his hand.

I'd never seen this guy before, and believe me, if I'd seen him, I would have remembered him.

He was old; not two steps from the grave old, but decades older than the rest of the people who worked here; especially older than the people in IT. Sure, there were a few exceptions. Sean was a good example. I knew he was probably in his late 50s, but based on the pictures I'd seen, he looked pretty much the same now as he did 20 years ago. It was what one software coder described as the "too many energy drinks, too many third shifts, too many 100-hour weeks, and too many impossible, arbitrary, deadlines syndrome." People in IT seemed to start out looking younger than everyone else, but quickly looked older than the rest. Most of the directors were in their 40s; the managers in their 30s, and the technicians ... the ones who actually did the work ... were in their 20s. It seemed like there were no old people who survived in IT.

The way this guy was dressed was bizarre, even for our IT department. He was wearing a suit, which is not uncommon for day-one new employees. For a moment, I was surprised that someone would wear a retro-vintage outfit to their first day at work. It was pure Disco era – vests, loud ties the size of dinner plates, and jacket lapels to match. I knew, because Jahmal had worn one to a company party last year, and was furious he had to spend most of the party explaining his costume to people. To top it all off, this guy was wearing a big, bushy mustache, the first one I'd ever seen at this company. Then it occurred to me that this wasn't some tongue-in-cheek homage to a long gone era. It may very well be what he thought was appropriate.

"Chris, good to see you." Sergiu gestured to the man with him, and said, "I'd like you to meet, Arthur ..."

"Art," the man cut off and corrected Sergiu in mid-sentence. "Just call me, Art."

Cutting off someone in mid-sentence was not a wise thing to do in this company, unless you outranked the speaker. So was this a new VP? I tried not to grin when the thought crossed my mind that he looked the part.

"Certainly," said Sergiu. "Chris, this is Art. This is his first day on-site, and I want you to let Art shadow you to help him get oriented."

Sergiu must have seen the puzzled look on my face, and after a moment of awkward silence added, "You must remember. It hasn't been that long since your manager assigned someone to do the same for you."

Nothing like that had ever happened with me. I'd been here less than a year, was on my third manager, if you didn't count our CIO Jessica as a temporary fill-in. None of them had ever talked about orientation with me. In fact, Ramesh, my hiring manager, had pulled me out of my HR form-filling session on day-one, and put me to work on a crisis right away.

I'd been short-changed. That was nothing new. My managers had ranged from those who always found fault with what I did, to those that didn't like me personally, to those who punished me solely to demonstrate to others they had the power to do so. I wasn't even sure the company hired managers who were actually interested in helping their team members advance.

It didn't matter. I'd accepted it, and wasn't going to let it show as a sign of my weakness. More importantly, Lee had called out that I didn't work well with others in my PIP, and refused to help others when they needed it. More lies, but clearly Sergiu didn't know that. This was just another test of my progress.

"Right … I'll be happy to get him started properly."

I reached out and shook his hand. "So, Arthur, what will you be doing here"?

"Please call me Art," he said, seeming a little annoyed. "Only my mother ever called me Arthur, and unless you're trying out for that role, just stick to, Art."

I gave it a polite laugh, and said, "Sorry. I won't forget again."

"So, its message received. Wonderful," added Sergiu, as he gathered papers from his desk. "Now, I don't mean to rush you out, but I have a meeting with our CIO, Jessica, in a few minutes. I'm going to ask you, Chris, to take the lead and handle this, okay"?

Without waiting for an answer, Sergiu walked around the desk, quickly shook Art's hand, and said, "Good luck," just before he walked out the door, leaving the two of us alone in his office.

"Well, Art," I said, strongly emphasizing his name, to let him know I got it. I waved my hand toward the door and said, "Shall we begin"?

I was surprised at how fast Art walked. My prejudices were showing through. I figured that with him being older, he'd just be slower on everything, but I was pressed to keep up with him.

"Turn right at the next corner. We'll stop in the break room," I said. "I'd like to pick up some coffee and thought you might like some too. We've got other beverages, too ... black teas, herbal teas, green teas ..."

Art cut me off in mid-sentence. It seemed like that was a habit of his. That was going to be a problem here in our culture. "Just give me a steaming hot cup of blood, black with four sugars."

I stopped and asked, "Blood"?

"Coffee," he snapped, and kept on walking.

I caught up with Art, just as he reached the coffee station. "What kind of coffee would you like"? I asked. "We have decaf, morning roast, seasonal blend, dark roast, and you can blend them any way you want."

Art scowled at me. "Do you know why we call coffee, 'Blood'"?

I shook my head.

"That's because of all the caffeine coursing through our veins. I don't want tea, and I don't want some aromatic blend. I want coffee, hot, black and four sugars, and I want it to have as much caffeine in it as possible."

"Okay. I prefer tea, but I'll get you something. Why don't you go grab a table, so we can chat for a moment, to make sure I get you to the right places for your new role"?

Art scowled, and marched off to a table. As I was filling a cup for him with some morning blend and some dark roast, I caught him out of the corner of my eye. He was impatiently drumming the table top with his fingers, almost as if he considered stopping to have a cup of coffee a frivolous indulgence.

I set the steaming brew down in front of him, and dropped packets of sugar and artificial sweeteners beside it. He grabbed four of the sugar packets, stacked them up, and broke them in half over his drink. I almost choked when he pulled a cheap, plastic pen out of his shirt pocket and used it to stir his coffee.

At my surprise, Art smiled for the first time since I'd met him and said, "I've been using this pen to stir my coffee for weeks. I'll keep doing it until it runs out of ink, and then I'll get a new one. Gives my coffee that special 'tang' I enjoy."

I laughed. If he had a sense of humor, no matter how strange, I could work with him. I'd always found that people without a sense of humor were not to be trusted. If they could laugh at themselves, then they could probably become friends.

While I waited for my Assam tea to finish brewing, I asked Art, "Tell me a little about yourself and your background."

"Is it relevant? I went through all that in the interviews with your leaders. Assume it's probably sufficient for the task at hand, and that you won't have me dragging you down."

I leaned across the table. "Because knowing your background will help me tailor what I show you, so as to minimize the waste of your time, and get you productive as quickly as possible."

Art nodded. "Makes sense." He took a large gulp of the steaming coffee. The coffee machine was set to keep coffee so hot it was barely cooler than the surface of the sun. I didn't understand how Art could swallow something that hot.

Art grimaced and said, "Kinda watery and weak. You need some real Navy coffee in here. Throw coffee and water into a pot, add a little salt, bring it to a roaring boil, and then it's ready. That's coffee which will put a kick in your backside."

"I'll make a note."

"You asked about my background. I won the Intel STS at 16. I hold bachelors and masters degrees in Manufacturing Production Engineering. I wrote a doctoral thesis on measurement and remediation of production variance in real time when I was 21, but never finished the program. Too much academic nonsense. Went to work in the automobile industry. Spent a few years there reducing their production costs and improving their quality. Left and spent some time writing two textbooks on the subject, and building in-house training tools. I believe in teaching companies to fish, rather than feeding them. If I can't help people the first time, then they shouldn't keep me around."

Art swallowed the rest of his coffee in one gulp. "I went to China for a while, to help them pilot a transition of their heavy industry production, to an operation that would go head to head against the best in the world, based on production quality, delivery and performance. Then I spent some time as a civilian contractor for the Department of Defense working on classified … "

The more Art went on, the more impressed I was. I had written him off on first sight, but this guy had more hands-on, real-world experience than almost anyone I had ever known … except maybe Sean. He was smart … really smart. The only problem was, it was not in our industry, or even relevant. It was about things that were antiques.

"That sounds really impressive, Art. What is the role here at the company you're going to be filling"?

"I don't fill roles. Never have. Filling roles is for chair-warmers, government workers, and those on in-house retirement … all those sinecure holders. I make things better by improving the quality, consistency and timeliness of what we manufacture. When I can't improve things any further, I move on."

He leaned across the table and jabbed his finger at me. "So should we all. Tell me, Chris. How do you make a difference? What do you do that makes this company better"?

I'd never been asked that question here, during an interview, or by a manager.

"Well, you see my role is complex. It involves …"

"You're fired," snapped Art.

My heart sank. How could that be? Was Art my even newer boss?

Art must have seen my dismay. "You're in luck. You don't work for me, so you're not fired. If you were on my staff, you'd be walking out the door with your personal effects in a box. How can you expect to partner with other teams, if you can't even tell them what you do, and how it will help them. If you don't know, why should they bother to find out?"

"I doubt there are many people here who could give you that information, that fast," I said. "Our work here is complex. This is a 21st century, service-oriented organization. A lot of our business is software and consulting services, that don't lend themselves to easy answers. Things continue to get more complex as time goes on." I didn't want to bring up that this is not the same business world as the auto industry probably had been, especially when I didn't know how it could bounce back at me.

Art shook his head. "The most complex thoughts and processes, when fully understood, are expressible in very simple ways. Think about Einstein's $E=mc^2$. When examined in detail, it reveals itself as truly complex, visionary, and insightful. Yet when summarized by someone who truly understands the complexity, it is so simple, that almost every schoolchild has knowledge of the equation."

Art stood up. "I'm not here to educate you. You are here to educate me. Shouldn't we proceed? You can bring your ... tea ... with you. We need to make better use of our time. That's what we're getting paid for."

I was not going to let Art take control of this assignment, and report that back to Sergiu, especially with me on a performance improvement plan. That would get me fired, for sure. Since Art seemed to have opinions on everything, I decided to use his strength to reassert control over him and this assignment. I'd see how smart he really was, by having him review the KPIs the experts at SMT gave us.

I stood up and said, "Follow me, please. I would like the benefit of your background and opinions on some things we are encountering here." I also made a mental note to create a synopsis of everything I did with Art, just in case Sergiu, or someone else, decided it was a good idea to start asking around about what I was doing to orient Art.

A few minutes later we were sitting in my cube.

I paged through the presentation to the section on KPIs, and then slid it across the desk to him. Unfortunately, that didn't stop him from going back to the beginning, and looking through it slide by slide.

"No ... no," I said. "That's the wrong spot. I want to show you where we are in terms of our Key Performance Indicators ... our KPIs ... that's where I would like to take advantage of your experience and training."

Art scowled at me and said, "Relax. I know what a KPI is. I was building business metrics before you could add."

"Those are just presentation slides for framing the KPI discussion. It's not intended to add ..."

"Material value"? interrupted Art. "Then why waste people's time with them"?

"You don't understand ..."

"A piece of free advice, Chris. Telling someone they 'don't understand,' is the same as saying they are right, you're wrong, and you don't have any way to respond other than punting."

I couldn't believe Art. I was responsible for orienting him, and unless I did something to get the situation back under control, he was going to be leading his own orientation.

"Art, it is different here than what you may be used to." I poked the KPI presentation documents with my finger. "Leaders in this company expect presentations to look, and feel, a certain way. If you do it differently, they get nervous, because they don't know what to expect. That's why we all follow this form. Surely with your background you can relate to standardization and consistency, not to mention that leaders hate looking ignorant, almost as much as they hate being surprised in public."

"Nothing ever remains the same forever. I'd have gone broke in a heartbeat if I kept producing last year's model car, no matter how high the quality and standardization."

I shook my head. "Perhaps it is a little different in our industry. Here, if I change and do it differently from everyone else, leadership is going to put me under a magnifying glass, and that is not a career advancing move anyplace I've ever worked."

"What are you afraid of? You're looking through the wrong end of the telescope. You've fallen for the old 'Learn Not to Burn by Keeping a Low Profile' method of career management, where survival is the only goal, even if it keeps you in the same job, or at the same level, forever. Doing it better is not about being different for its own sake. It's about improving the company, by saving leadership's time, and helping them focus on the key decisions that need to be made. Business is a complex and dynamic environment. That means it constantly changes, and if we aren't getting better, we are failing."

Nice theory, I thought to myself. More likely a great way to get fired. Art just didn't understand how things worked here. He was still stuck in the old ways, when there were more jobs than people. Today, there were more people for each job every year, and as you went up in the organization, it only got worse. If you raised your head up too high, it got cut off by somebody else on their way up. The new business reality had arrived, and he was still stuck 20 years ago.

"Thanks for the feedback," I said. "I'll re-look at how I'm presenting the information. But that doesn't change anything about the KPIs. I still want your feedback."

I opened the presentation back to the section listing out the KPIs, and pushed the documents back in front of him. I was not going to give in on this.

Tips that would have helped Chris

You won't know everything you need to know

You may not have full awareness of all aspects of an ITSM initiative, beyond the minimum you need to accomplish your elements of it. This is especially true for highly confidential initiatives, or those where the subject could cause undue concern among employees or investors. It is reasonable to ask for additional information, but sometimes you must trust your leaders' opinions of how much information to provide you.

Know what you do

If you cannot articulate what you do, and how it drives benefits for the company, in simple, direct language that anyone inside or outside the company can understand, then you don't know what you do. No job is that complicated. If you don't know what you do, you will find it very hard to convince others to work with you.

Know when to bend the rules

To succeed and advance, you must stand out from your peers. That usually means doing some things differently. Don't do them differently just for the sake of being different. Do them differently because it yields substantial benefits to the organization.

CHAPTER 6: EVERY JOURNEY BEGINS WITH A DESTINATION

Art shook his head, and then pulled a pair of reading glasses from his shirt pocket and started to read. After a moment, he pulled a mechanical pencil out of that same pocket. He gave the pencil two clicks, and without asking, began making either an "X" or a "Checkmark," beside each KPI.

"Yes ... No ... No ... No ... Yes ..." Art stopped, and looked up at me, his pencil's tip frozen to a KPI on the list. "Are you kidding me? Did you even look at these? Where did you get them? Please tell me you didn't create them"?

I grabbed the SMT performance management module instruction book, all 423 pages of it, and dropped it on the table in front of Art. It made a resounding thud when it landed.

"These are the KPIs that the experts at SMT designed as part of their tool development. SMT has a committee of over a dozen business experts dedicated to the identification and maintenance of the best KPIs. In fact, they play a major role working with the international standards organizations, establishing best practices for companies around the globe. These are the best of the best, state of the art, modern KPIs," and I emphasized the word, "Modern," to ensure Art got it.

"Okay, who is this set of so-called modern measures intended for"? asked Art.

"They're for everyone," I said, jabbing the sheet with my finger. I wasn't sure what Art's "X" and "Checkmark" code meant, and I didn't really care, so I poked at them all.

"Everything you need to know about the activities of the service desk," I said. "It makes no sense to pre-select who can see which measure. What if the CFO has a concern that could be easily resolved by knowing something about the turnover rate in service technicians? That's not a finance measure. Successful, modern corporations think horizontally, not just vertically. The challenges of business don't fit neat and tightly into one functional area. By making all of these available in an executive dashboard, we give leaders and operational managers the consistent and aligned information they need to answer any question, and follow any question, no matter where it leads. There is nothing more empowering than self-service."

"Interesting approach," said Art, as he closed the presentation up.

Perhaps I had cracked some of his code. All I needed to do was aggressively stand up to him, and then he would listen to me.

Before I could enjoy my new found success, Art grinned, and added, "Had any luck with it working? Has leadership bought in to your argument"?

"Leadership is fully engaged. They gave me a lot of good feedback. That's what I'm doing now, incorporating their feedback into further revisions. That's the way I get their commitment to the solution. That's the way they invest some skin in the game. Far better to have them in my camp complaining, than outside and against me."

"Did they like the measures"?

"It's not a question of liking, or not liking, the measures. As I said before, these are the best of the best KPIs. SMT has seen to that."

"I bet you believe in unicorns too."

"That's uncalled for," I insisted.

"Well I believe in them. You ought to try it," said Art with a laugh. I tried hard not to laugh but couldn't keep it down.

"Seriously," he said. "Look at some of these metrics." Art drew a line down the margin of the list of SMT KPIs.

"How about this one ... 'Time to resolve incidents.' Did you ...'"?

"Yes, that's a great example of a KPI important to both operational efficiency and leadership decision making." I cut Art off before he could continue. That wasn't good. I was starting to pick up his bad habits.

"Okay, but what does it measure, and why is that anything more than a simple measurement ... a metric of some minimal interest outside the IT operational departments? Who else needs to know"?

"You're joking, aren't you? Restoration after incidents directly impacts our ability to consistently deliver services to our users. They will want to know."

Art shook his head. "Ah-ha. I see your error. You are confusing communication with metrics," he said. "It's easy for rookies to get confused, as they both require measurements, but those same values are used for very different things, have different audiences, and have different levels of importance."

Art gave me a condescending look, like I were some kind of a simpleton. "The difference between five minutes and five hours to restore service based on an incident, rarely has anything to do with the type of incident. There are too many other factors. Don't worry about your mistake," he said. "Everyone makes it. You're just fortunate I'm here. I'll help you."

I was really beginning to dislike Art, with his constant air of superiority.

"Art, these are analytics," I said. "They are numbers, values that measure performance. If it takes me an average of two hours to restore service after an incident, then it takes me two hours. It's an objective fact, and even if SMT hadn't identified it as one of the critical KPIs, anyone with any understanding ..."

"It doesn't mean beans. It is not ... I repeat, not a KPI for leadership. However, it does have limited value as a metric for the ..."

At that moment, Sean walked into my cube. I stifled a laugh. This was going to be good. Sean, the original old-school sarcastic UNIX expert meets Art, mister by the book old school manufacturing expert. I gave them about two minutes before they were down on the floor trying to kill each other. This was going to be fun. My money was on Sean.

"Sean, have you met Art"? I asked. "He's new here and ..."

Art stood up and shoved his hand toward Sean. "And Chris has graciously agreed to show me around and get me off to a good start." Sean stared at Art's extended arm for a moment, as if he were not quite sure what he was supposed to do, then stepped back, pressed his palms together in front of the center of his chest, and gave a slight bow, while saying, "Namaste."

Art smiled, and pulled his hand back, stood straight up, and held his hands together in a gesture that looked like what Sean had done, except his hands were much higher. The tips of his fingers were nearly touching his chin. He performed a deeper bow than Sean had, and said, "Sawasdee."

Both men faced each other in a moment of silence, then smiled as if they had just met an old friend. I had no idea what had just happened, but my instincts told me I had just seen two grand masters of one-upmanship using a challenge to assess their opponent's capabilities. I mentally kicked myself for not recording this first round on my phone, so I could upload them to the Internet later. This was going to be really fun to watch. I kept thinking about that alleged quote from a famous general who, upon making contact with the best his opponent had to offer, told his aide that finally they had someone worthy of fighting. I only wish I knew who had won that round.

Art waited until Sean sat down, before returning to his seat as before.

Sean turned to Art and said, "What kind of falsehoods and nonsense has Chris been telling you"?

"I've been explaining the difference between metrics and KPIs to him," said Art. "Just starting to help Chris better understand the difference and where to apply them. Next we're going to explore the differences between mathematics and statistics."

Sean looked at me and shook his head. "Good luck. After you do that, there is this little problem called, 'World Hunger,' it should be a snap compared to educating Chris."

"Don't talk about me in the third person, like I'm not even here. Sean, you think the average time to resolve incidents is a critical KPI, don't you"?

I was so confident Sean would agree with me, I treated it like a rhetorical statement, rather than a question.

Sean shrugged. "It depends. Generally, it's not. The difference between 10 minutes and 10 hours can be as simple as the day of the week, or time of day."

I was flabbergasted.

"Look," said Sean. "It isn't a very good predictive indicator. It's like the roll of the dice, or the spin of a slot machine. Each situation is unique."

Art waited until Sean finished, and said, "I had an insurance company as a client one time, that wrote a lot of automobile insurance. They used to say with virtually identical circumstances, causes and factors, the difference between a hundred dollar claim and a million dollar claim can often be as little as sitting three inches one direction or another."

"So you're saying that the time it takes to recover from an incident has no information value"? I reached up and pulled down from my shelves SMT manuals and a host of books on ITSM best practices. "You're telling me that all of these experts are wrong and you two … " I wanted to put some nasty adjectives in, but held back. "You two are right, and they are not? Really? What do you say when the users and customers call, yelling at how long it takes us to restore service"?

"No, they are all right, even when they disagree," said Sean. "It's all a question of what normal means. You've got a speedometer on your car that has numbers, but no measure of what it relates to. It may say 60. But is that miles per hour ... kilometers per day ... furlongs per fortnight ... minutes till you arrive? It says nothing about whether it is good or bad. Suppose it is a nice, sunny, dry day, and you are driving 60 miles per hour on a new, well maintained, superhighway? That may be fine. If you're driving 60 miles per minute, you are being reckless. Or suppose you are in the middle of a raging blizzard on a poorly maintained, dirt road? Even 60 yards per hour may be too fast for safety."

I shook my head. "So you're telling me it's about context"? I was getting really confused.

"Yes," said Sean. "More importantly, what is the goal of that KPI? What strategy element are you trying to monitor? It's not about the actions you take as a result of one measure failing in one period. Those efforts are important to mitigate tactical damage to the user, but what outcomes will change, or you need to modify as a result."

"Every KPI should be tied to a strategic element that is integrated with the other KPIs, just not in a bunch of weasel-worded strategy statements. It needs to be crisp and clear. Like your 'time to restore service.' What level of restoration are you talking about? Do you have a minimum, accepted level of performance, or does that mean 100%? What's the difference to the business if it is only 80% of pre-incident functionality? Is that good enough"? said Art.

Having them both talking at me, was like trying to have two telephone conversations at the same time. "Are you trying to tell me that KPIs are part of my Service Level Agreement, my SLA? That's crazy."

Art nodded, then turned to Sean. "Let's give Chris some space to process all this. I don't want his head to explode ... at least not on my first day on-site."

They both laughed. I wasn't sure why, but at this point I was confident I was the butt of their joke. This was becoming a complete failure for me.

I started to speak, but Art cut me off saying, "Look, Chris, why don't you think about this for a while, and I'll spend some time with Sean. We can swap stories about who punched the most computer cards while in college."

They both laughed, and I hated it.

I tried to think of a good retort, but before I could speak, they both headed off to the break room, and I was left feeling ignorant and not very intelligent.

Tips that would have helped Chris

The significant few versus the trivial many

The hard part about assembling a best practice set of KPIs, or a governance dashboard, is not finding things to measure. It's about figuring out how to separate the significant few from the trivial many. Any measure will give you some kind of insight. The question is, will it give you insight that is greater than the cost, potential confusion, and fog associated with more measurements? Far more KPI efforts fail from too many measures, rather than too few.

Kindred spirits are everywhere

People connect and communicate when they have links of common interests or experience. Helping people find those links, will create stronger teams for you. When you make assumptions about people's interests, and compartmentalize people based on those assumptions, you prevent them from working together more effectively. Don't bias people against each other before they first connect. Let people come as they are.

CHAPTER 7: FRIEND OR FOE?

I never heard from Art and Sean again that day. I passed by the break room a while later, but they weren't there. I didn't even want to imagine where they had wandered, or what was amusing them. It was past my normal quitting time, so I did a habitual end of the day quick check of my calendar for tomorrow, before shutting everything down. It was a good thing I did.

Sergiu had sent a meeting invitation for first thing in the morning in his office with Art and me, to get an update on our progress. When you are on a performance improvement plan, failing at something like orienting a new employee ... something that everyone else would imagine to be easy enough for a child to do it ... you have absolutely no right to expect anything other than immediate termination. If Art gave him an honest account of what happened today, and Sergiu saw how Art had no respect for me, or my work, I'd be out the door with a box of my personal effects before lunch. Despite my good intentions and best efforts, I was failing in my assignment from Sergiu. Maybe I didn't have what it took to do this job after all.

For a moment I thought about gathering up my effects now, and stashing them in the trunk of my car, just in case. That way I wouldn't have to do the "box walk of failure" past everyone tomorrow. Right now, I didn't care. I was too mentally exhausted from trying to wrestle Art into line. It was like having two Seans at the same time.

As I walked through the parking lot, I tried to draw some satisfaction that I had made it through another day. Tomorrow was another opportunity to get things back under control and moving forward. It was the most positive thing I could think of.

When I got to my car, I realized one of my tires was flat.

I opened the trunk and pulled out the spare. I jerked it free and let it fall to the ground. It landed with a thud and no bounce. It was flat too. That was my fault. I couldn't remember the last time I'd checked it, but knowing that didn't make me feel any better. I just hoped my cell phone had enough battery left in it for me to call for a tow.

I ran a red light on my way to work the next morning. The only thing that kept me from getting a ticket was that the cop already had someone pulled over, so he wasn't paying attention. After getting a tow and a repair last night, I hadn't gotten home until late, but I'd spend a lot of hours putting together a presentation for Sergiu, identifying the areas that I'd already covered with Art, and my plans going forward. It was a good plan ... very comprehensive and very appropriate for a new employee. It seemed like the best defense to my failures of the previous day, and was a good offense identifying what I was planning to do in the future.

I was still confused about what they had been saying yesterday. The whole idea of a strategy for a KPI seemed like a lot of nonsense work. Anyone could see what needed to be measured, and with the predefined list of measures from SMT, it struck me as being nothing more than a waste of time.

When I reached my cube, the message light was flashing on my phone. I hesitated, and checked the time. I didn't want to be late for my meeting with Sergiu, but at the same time the call might be important and would only take a minute.

I dialed in the voicemail and was surprised when I heard Sergiu's voice telling me our meeting had been postponed, and that I was to join Art at the service desk facility for a meeting with Molly, because this was the only time she had available. He wanted me to get Art introduced and oriented with Molly, to ensure we were all on the same page. It was more checking on my PIP failings about not working well with others.

I quickly walked back to the parking lot. This was a terrible sign. Not only had I failed to get Art through very much yesterday, I now had my boss arranging my day for me. It seemed as if there was nothing I could do on my own.

I walked into the lobby of the service desk facility. Art was sitting in a chair up against the one wall, writing in a notebook. It looked like he was using that same pen he'd stirred his coffee with yesterday. He'd pulled the chair beside him around in front of his chair, and was using it as a flat surface to hold his folders and notebooks. Rearranging the furniture in the building lobby was not something one did at this company. Art needed to be careful, or he would get bounced out before my PIP was over. For an instant I wondered if that might not be a good idea. If only I could write a PIP about him, as Lee had done to me.

At Art's feet were stacked three empty, disposable coffee cups and one half-full one. I almost laughed when I saw the poster behind him on the wall. It was a recycle-reuse message which was part of one of the major company initiatives to be more environmentally responsible this year.

"Art, glad to see you. How are you doing"?

He looked up, holding his place in the notebook with his pen. He checked his watch and said, "Another five minutes and I would have done this myself."

"How did you find the service desk building, given that it is only your second day here and the building is unmarked"?

He unfolded a paper napkin with a drawing on it, and held it up for me to see. "Sean gave me directions after we talked with Sergiu and Jessica last night. Well, that's not really true. Sean was there with me having a beer, but it was my call and conversation."

"Last night? When"?

"Sometime after you went home. We would have asked you to come with us, but it seems you went home before everyone else. Not a good thing to do when you are on a PIP would be my advice. I called Sergiu at home last night to give him a quick update, so we wouldn't need to waste time meeting today. While we were on the phone, Jessica called Sergiu, and when she found out what we were talking about, Sergiu just conferenced her in. No sense in adding another layer to the communication. It just wastes time."

I stood in front of Art, totally stunned. This just wasn't done ... especially not on your first day at work. How was he getting away with this? If I even tried that kind of behavior, I'd get fired. What kind of feedback had he given Sergiu and Jessica? Had he told them what really went on, and how little we accomplished? I'd never even gotten to present my own defense.

Art scowled at me and said, "Relax. I've never seen anyone so in fear for their job before. If Sergiu or Jessica had been so upset about what I said that they wanted to fire you immediately, don't you think they would have had HR and security cut you off at your cube this morning"?

Art was right … again … as usual. I was really beginning to hate him for that.

Before I could say anything in response, the doorway from the lobby into the facility slammed open, and Molly came running out.

She looked at me and then turned to Art, "You're both here, good. Are you ready to …"?

Molly froze for an instant, and all the energy seemed to flow out of her, as if she saw something about Art she hadn't expected.

I pointed to Art and said, "Hi Molly. Good to see you again." I gestured toward Art and said, "I'd like you to meet …"

She cut me off and extended her hand. "Art, yes I know. We've met before."

Art's expression never changed. "Good to see you again, Molly. Hope you are doing well."

In an instant, it was over, and Molly was back to her normal, perky self. "Then let's go get started."

The heavy soundproofing was evident when Molly closed the door to her office, and the incessant din from the service representatives disappeared. I reveled in the soundproofed quiet of Molly's office for a moment, while standing in front of a wall of glass, and watching the rows of representatives appear to silently field customer calls. Directly opposite her desk was a wall of monitors giving real-time updates in charts, and the number of calls in queue, abandoned call rates, average call time, and a number of other key performance indicators for the day, the week and the month. That was why we were here.

Without waiting to be invited, Art sat down in a chair directly in front of Molly's desk, and rearranged some of the things on her desk, so he could lay out his notebook and folders. Molly frowned, but Art didn't seem to pick up on it. If he did, he chose to ignore it.

"I'm so glad you could adjust your schedules and meet me now," said Molly. "I really appreciate your flexibility."

"Thanks," I said. "We're here so we can get introduced and understand what we are trying to accomplish, and how the service desk can be an example for other organizations to model in the development of KPIs. I really appreciate your ..."

Art cut me off. "Actually, we're here to take a look at your measures ... your metrics, and determine the alignment with those in the SMT tool, and those that are also useful to the company. Then we will know where you need to make adjustments."

Art was definitely not subtle, and he was definitely abrasively offensive.

"I'm happy to go through any of our KPIs with you," said Molly, ignoring Art's denigrating comments. She quickly called up historical trending charts and data onto the monitors on her walls, replacing the real-time measures currently displayed.

Satisfied she had the right elements displayed; Molly got up from behind her desk and walked to the monitors. Molly seemed to be more comfortable ... more confident, when she was up and moving, as if sitting behind a desk were a prison for her. She pointed to the first monitor and began to explain it to us. It displayed a series of three dimensional ribbon charts for each of 10 measures over the last few months, on a week by week basis, against their performance expectations. The numerical values for each measure were contained in a large data grid, directly under the graphs. Each value in the grid was color coded based on its value. It was almost overwhelming in its thoroughness.

"Each data point on this chart represents one week's results in meeting our performance standards. Measures that exceeded performance commitments by at least 10% are green. Measures that merely met the performance commitments are yellow, and those that failed to meet their commitments are in red. As you can see from this historical chart, our performance in each of the 10 most important measures has exceeded our commitments, every week, by at least 10%. In fact, the performance of this team has not only exceeded our commitments, it has remained consistent over the entire time-frame. I'm very proud of our team."

"That's very impressive," I said. "Can you please tell us what is on the ..."?

Art interrupted. "Before we move on to other areas and start handing out awards, I have some questions. I've got three comments about the mechanics of the charts. First, they are practically illegible because of all the chart junk on them. Drop that 3D effect. It has no place in business. Save it for the movies. Second, decide if you want a data table of numbers or a chart. You don't need both. And third, don't just show me lines or numbers. Show me conclusions and recommendations. What actions should I take based on these results? It doesn't matter whether you are a C-level executive or a line supervisor, no one can get anything useful from this chart other than as a piece of abstract art."

Molly's attitude never seemed to change. She remained positive and upbeat despite Art's attack.

She smiled at Art and said, "I know you just arrived here, Art. I also know that you are very intelligent and experienced, so you will understand why this company places a priority on using the tools and reports from the SMT system without customization. I'm sure you've seen the chaos that results when you do otherwise; how it becomes impossible to upgrade, and ultimately you spend more of your time trying to keep the system from crashing, rather than using it to provide information for decision makers."

Gesturing at the charts displayed on the monitors, Molly added, "These are part of the standard report set that comes with the SMT tool. Is it perfect? Of course not. Nothing ever is. However, it does provide information for people that prefer to look at data this way, versus a written summary. More importantly, it is what the service desk teams are now accustomed to. The disruptive effect on our users of changing their behavior for some cosmetic alterations in how a chart is presented, is simply not worth it at this time. You know that. You know there are more important issues in play here now."

Art dismissed her comment with a wave of his hand. "It is your area to manage, Molly. Do whatever you want. Just understand that I am trying to help you with some perspective and suggestion. Better for me to point out the wasting of resources on activities that add no value, than to have leadership do the same. You know how that would look. Regardless, can you simply show us what you think your KPIs are, and what their values have been"? With a slightly sarcastic tilt to his voice, he added, "Can you possibly do that without violating that questionable rule about customization"?

"Not a problem," said Molly, still not showing any response to Art and his aggressive approach. "Just give me a minute to whip up an ad hoc report especially for you. I must reiterate that there is a great deal of evidence that not customizing is the best path in the long run."

A legible data table appeared on the monitor. Every KPI measure exceeded its goal by at least 10%. It appeared that there had never been a yellow warning, much less a service breach, over the entire measured timeframe. There was nothing of note, except rows of green numbers for each of the measures. As Molly paged through the 27 different measures, very little changed.

Finally, Molly brought us back at the first screen. Without looking up, she said, "These are some of the most important metrics to running a good service desk for your users, which is why it is at the beginning. It has tried and true measures like mean time to answer, and percentage of calls to abandoned; measures that virtually every service desk uses, and you will note that we are over-performing in every case."

Molly gestured out through the glass wall to the rows of desks and service representatives responding to user calls, and said, "I'd stack this service desk team up against any I've ever worked with. Look at that performance. Have you ever seen a service desk team … "?

Art cut her off. "Doing such a miserable job, and the worst part is, neither they nor their management realize it. Which means there is no way they are ever going to get any better."

I jumped in. Art was not going to run this show as he did yesterday. "Art, these charts show how the service desk is doing a great job and we should be ..."

Art cut me off. "We should be concerned that the measures have been solidly green for so long."

"What's wrong with green? Don't you want to see success"? I asked.

"I want success more than you can know," said Art. "But more than that, I want reality. If this team has never had to adjust to reality at any time, it tells me something will be out of alignment, and will have been that way for some time. Unfortunately, because it's been invisible to us, we've only let it get worse, and eventually it will fail in a big way ... in a way that will hurt our users."

"What"? snapped Molly. "You think it's good if my team fails? Are you crazy"?

Art shook his head. "No, not crazy. Just try to help them succeed ... really succeed, not just track a number. And succeed in a way that doesn't waste company resources, and gives users what they want."

Molly said nothing, but she was clearly upset, too angry to say anything. It looked like Art had finally found her weak spot.

"Thank you," said Molly, as Art collected his notebook and materials. It had been a brutal hour, with Art attacking Molly's team and performance measures at every junction, while Molly reacted as the consummate professional. She refused to respond in kind, merely nodding at his assertions, and continuing to present her team in the best light possible.

Art and I stood up together. Without waiting for me, he headed out. He had just opened the door when Molly said, "Chris, will you stay behind for a few minutes, I want to follow up with you on that other project we were working on. I can get someone to help Art find his way back to the lobby."

"I hardly need someone to help me with something so trivial," said Art. "Chris and I came in separate cars, and I am capable of traveling on my own. I have too much to do. Unless of course, Chris feels the need for assistance in finding his way back home."

Molly spoke up before I could. "Don't worry, I'll make sure Chris finds his way out."

Without even a goodbye, Art left and closed the door behind him.

Molly and I stood silently for a moment before I said, "What project are you talking about. I don't know anything about another project"?

"There is no other project," said Molly. "I needed to talk to you without Art."

"Why"?

"You seem like a good person who has the best interest of the company, its employees, and its customers at heart. That's why you should know that I have worked with companies before at the same time Art was there, and I think that you should be very wary of him."

"What do you mean? Sure he is annoying, but so are lots of people."

"That's not what I mean. Has he told you why he is here"?

"He's a new employee. Sergiu asked me to help orient him as part of my PIP."

Molly shook her head. "I think you were lied to by omission. As far as I know, Art is a consultant, not an employee."

"What? I'll have to check with Sergiu and Art when I get back to the main building."

"I wouldn't advise that," she said. "If Art hasn't told you, he doesn't want you to know. The fact that Sergiu hasn't told you, suggests they are in league together. You are on a PIP, so if they suspect you are on to them, you may be out of here immediately."

"Then what do you suggest I do"?

"Do what you've been asked. Work your way off the PIP. Just know that things are not as they seem. Your job, and the jobs of many others at your company, may be at risk. I can't tell you more at the risk of my own situation. If my employer found out, I'd be fired. We are not supposed to do anything that could jeopardize the successful conclusion of our business arrangement with your company."

"I don't understand."

Molly walked over to the door. She opened it, and the cacophony from all those service representatives taking calls filled the room.

I walked to the door. Standing in the doorway with me, Molly said, "Just be careful, and find out why he is here. Don't let ignorance blind you. That's all I will say."

As her door closed behind me and I headed back to the lobby, I wondered if there was any truth to her comments, or if she was just upset at the way he attacked her team's results. And if she were correct, what did that mean about the tasks Sergiu was giving me?

Tips that would have helped Chris

KPIs need a purpose

KPIs are tracked for many reasons. Unfortunately, very few of them are tracked for the right reason. KPIs are not just about reporting a number. They are about measuring progress towards an objective, via the critical success factors necessary to make it happen.

Whispers are dangerous

When a person takes you into their confidence for the purpose of warning you that someone you are working with is not to be trusted, it creates a challenging situation. You need to ask yourself why they are sharing this with you. It may be because they are trying to help you. It may be because they are working an unrelated agenda involving that person. Or it may even be to damage you professionally. While it is appropriate to be appreciative and gracious about the extension of trust, make sure you consider all the possibilities before you act. Remember the con artist. They will always extend you their trust first. They know that you do not get trust unless you give trust.

7: Friend or Foe?

You can't control all lines of communication

Some people think they can manage initiatives by controlling all lines of communication, so they try to manage what is said and to whom. In practice, this is impossible to accomplish. For example, others may talk to your manager about you, and about your work, or your manager may talk to them about the same things; all outside of your presence and awareness. You cannot control those dialogues, so don't try. Run your initiative transparently, so that there will be no content in those conversations that you have not already shared with the relevant parties. Knowledge is like water. It wants to be free. You can hinder its path, but in the end, it will become free. Rather than trying to prevent it, embrace it. Use it to your advantage, and build a reputation as an honest, straightforward practitioner who keeps people informed, and doesn't try to hide things.

CHAPTER 8: HUNTERS AND GATHERERS

I'd started off trying to meet with Danesh, the director over the people who managed the company's data repositories, and was also responsible for the company's efforts in the implementation of operation of the SMT system. That had gone nowhere. I couldn't even get past his administrative assistant, especially when I tried to communicate what I wanted to meet about. She gave me a lot of creative excuses, but I knew the reality.

He wasn't interested in meeting with me for three reasons. First, I was at a lower level in the organization, and meeting with me would not help him in the eyes of his peers and leaders; second, I was interested in what he considered tactical operational matters, rather than policy and direction; and third, I was interested in SMT, which he viewed as an insult to his team and their ability to build something similar to exactly match the needs of the company, instead of spending all that cash to buy something from a vendor that didn't quite fit.

The best I could get was some time with Berdina, one of his direct reports. More importantly, she had the tactical and operational accountability for assisting the vendor in enabling the tool. Ultimately, she'd own managing the operation of the tool. In other words, if you wanted to do anything with the SMT tool, or get any data out of it, it had to pass her approval.

Her office was neat and precise, with everything arranged in sparse, clean lines. Everything seemed to be in a place designed exactly for it. Berdina appeared to blend right in. Tall, blonde, with narrow, blue eyes, she had almost a gaunt line to her face. The one thing in her office that stood out as personal, was a small, carved wooden statue of Ganesha, in the back of her cube, sitting beside her computer terminal. It looked like a vacation souvenir.

There were a few personal items on the walls of the cube, mostly photographs of what seemed to be friends. One that jumped out was a large group photo. It looked like a gathering of sun-burnt tourists, with what appeared to be a younger Berdina standing beside them, and dressed in what almost looked like a uniform. They seemed to be standing in front of what looked like some relief carvings at the Borobudur Temple complex in Java. I recognized the location, because my sister had sent me a postcard with an almost identical picture, from her vacation a few years ago.

Berdina stood up when I entered her cube.

I extended my hand and said, "Thank you very much for agreeing to meet with me. I know you must be very busy."

Berdina gave a polite smile, then said, "It is my pleasure," and sat down without shaking my hand. "How may I assist you today"? she asked.

"I couldn't help but notice you had a statue of Ganesha next to your computer. I suppose everyone needs all the help we can get when dealing with machines. Your work must be very challenging. I don't know how you do it every day."

"It was a gift from a friend from home. While I appreciate your support for my labors, we are not here to talk about them. What can I do to assist you"?

"I noticed that picture," I said, pointing to the group photo on the wall. "Isn't that the Borobudur Temple complex?

Did you go there on vacation? My sister went to Java a few years ago and sent me a postcard of that same area."

"I was born in Java. My family originally came from the Netherlands, but they have lived in Java for several generations. We have substantial business interests on the island." She pointed to the picture. "That picture was taken some time ago. I was working a summer job as a docent in the temple complex. Who knows, perhaps your sister was in one of my tour groups. I came here when I went to college, and elected to remain after graduation."

Berdina turned back to me, "Is this why you asked to meet with me, to inventory and evaluate the contents of my office? I have a holder for tissues in my desk drawer which was a present from my sister. Would you like to inspect that too? Surely you have a more important reason for taking up my time like this"?

"Sorry. I was just trying to be friendly. I like to know something about the people I am working with."

"Let us base the nature of our relationship on the success with which we achieve our common goals, and not our diverse personal histories," she added tersely.

"Agreed," I said. "We've been working with Molly in the service desk, trying to get a handle on the Key Performance Indicators she is using, understanding why she is using them, and if there are better alternatives."

Berdina shook her head. "The governance group for the SMT tool has decided that there will be no customization of the tool from a workflow or data collection standpoint. The report writer has the capability to produce different types of reports, but the source data is fixed."

"I'm glad to hear you have a governance effort. Who is represented on it"?

"The governance group consists of members of my team," said Berdina. "We evaluated the types of issues the governance group would need to deal with, and decided that they would be too complex for users and other non-specialists to evaluate. Governance is a critical item, but unless the group responsible for it can be knowledgeable enough about the technology to make informed decisions, it will only waste time, and delay service to the users. That's why my team manages the SMT governance for the rest of the company. No one understands the application as well as we do."

"Then who speaks to the needs and interests of the users? How are they represented"? I asked.

"We have found, through very painful experience, that listening to the users can be a huge mistake. They often think they know what they want, but fail to bound it within the world of what's possible. They often don't know what they want, only what they have had before. They need gentle guidance, and that is part of my role, to see that they get what they truly need, not what they want."

"I see." This seemed to fly in the face of what I had learned before; that if IT failed to respond to the user, then they were not going to provide what was needed, and would end up being seen as a failure in the eyes of their users.

I reminded myself of the lesson I had learned before. It's not a good idea to try and change people's minds when you are still gathering facts. If you do, the information flow to you will stop there, and the conversation will degrade into a dialogue about who is right or wrong.

"Thank you for that insight. I'd never thought of it that way. I have another question for you. Where does the data used for analysis by SMT come from? What's the source? Is it something new, or was it around before the SMT tool was installed"?

Berdina looked at me as if I had three heads. "You're kidding, aren't you"?

I didn't want to look stupid, so I said, "I just need to verify for our records. I didn't want to bias your response by anything I said."

Redolent with the boredom from reciting her answer a thousand times before, Berdina said, "SMT is the primary data source, especially for the types of things that interest the service desk. All of the contacts they get regarding incidents, requests, and other items, are based on data entered into the TMP system by the operational teams, and the people raising the issues, whether they are users or members of the service desk."

"So you're telling me all the TMP system does is report back out on the data we put into it"?

"That's overly simplistic. There are data feeds from the automated configuration discovery, as well as asset and financial inputs. However, at a high level, as far as the service desk is concerned, you are correct."

I shook my head. "I think I am confused. If all it does is report back on what we put in, why all the restrictions? In fact, why do we even need to use it at all"?

Berdina closed her eyes and took a deep breath. Clearly, I was not the first person to have asked this question, although I'm sure she hoped I would be the last. It couldn't be fun spending your time justifying the acquisition and use of a tool that you felt was sub-standard, and that you could build better if the company only had more faith in you.

Without even opening her eyes, almost as if she were reading the words off the inside of her eyelids, Berdina said, "The tool allows us to track everything that happens to each request or incident, and allows for an orderly execution of processes and procedures necessary to ensure all of the appropriate steps are taken to restore, or enhance, service to our customers. While some information, such as existing asset data and financial charging rates, comes from external sources, it is appropriate as an operational construct to understand the data flows."

It even sounded like a typical, canned, mission statement. In other words, the quality of what came out of the system, was only as good as the integrity and consistency of the data that went in. I wondered why no one had thought of that, but then realized they probably did, but didn't really care, because in their minds it was the natural order of the relationship between IT and the users.

"It sounds like you have a tight handle on the information flow. How do you handle all of the data streams? Obviously, they have their own natural cycles, with one type of data coming in monthly, another weekly, some others daily. How do you reconcile them"?

Berdina tapped the tip of her index finger on the desk. "The answer is quite simple. We sample whatever data we have collected on a monthly basis. That way we don't have to worry about keeping track of all of the different points in time data becomes available. We simply look at the data on a monthly basis, and take it as we find it."

"Doesn't that mean you'll be taking some data midway through its cycle, so what you collect may not accurately reflect what's going on, or be aligned with the other data"?

She shook her head. "The consistency of monthly sampling effectively neutralizes that concern. Being consistent is far more important to our reporting templates than identifying what data is available when. If we don't align to the reporting templates we've defined, we run the risk of not being able to supply the users with the right set of reports, at the right time; and serving the user is our most important concern."

It didn't sound that way to me. It sounded more and more as if Berdina did things in a way that satisfied the needs of her team first, and the user second ... not through any bad intent, rather, just through a view of the role of the relationship between IT and the user.

"What about the reporting"? I asked. "I see there is a list of canned reports ..."

Berdina cut me off. "Yes, the governance group determined these would be the best reports for the users. They would provide the users with the information most useful to them. However, we were not so stupid as to think that they might never need another different report. That is why we established a process and procedure whereby they can request a new ad hoc report."

She rummaged through a drawer in her desk for a moment, and then produced a sheet of paper. She slid it across the table towards me. It was a form with spaces to fill out what you wanted for a new report, why the existing reports could not provide adequate information, and how long you wanted to receive the report, as well as lines for approvals of the request.

"Once the user completes the information, it is reviewed by the governance group at their regular monthly meeting. If it has merit, and fulfils a need the governance group feels the existing reports are not currently meeting, then it is routed for business approval and financial funding by the user's manager. Once that is obtained, work begins on development of the new report. This way we can be highly responsive to the rapidly changing needs of the business, and provide a high level of service to our users."

"About how long does it take to do all of this"? I asked.

"No two situations are the same. In the past, we have averaged between six and eight weeks from approval of the request, to delivery of report to the user."

"What if the users need the report sooner"?

"It is incumbent on the users to plan ahead for what they need. It's important to understand that we may be developing other reports which might provide the user with sufficient functionality that the new report might be unnecessary. We don't want to burden the SMT system with needless reports. If that isn't soon enough, there is a report writer in the tool itself."

"So users can develop their own ad hoc reports"? This seemed like the first user-focused item Berdina had mentioned so far.

"Yes, although users don't take advantage of it very much, so they are apparently quite happy with the existing reports we provide."

It didn't take long for me to figure out that this was the report writer that came with the application. From what I'd been told, it was written by, and for, technical specialists. Unless you knew all of the right technical terms and data labels, it took forever to generate even a simple report. Even then it was obtuse, and you never knew if it contained all the information you were looking for.

It seemed really strange that a group of engineers, people who are focused on specifics and measurement, should decide they are all graphic designers with advanced training in human factors, whenever it came to developing user outputs or report writing tools. Turn them loose, and before you knew it, there would be unintelligible 3D charts with shadows and perspective which used every bit of visual eye candy in the applications tool sets. It was so bad that I would not have been even a little surprised to see a chart with an animated dancing elf in the corner doing an interpretive dance, to illustrate the information produced by the data.

"Have you ever considered soliciting input from users, and revisiting the catalog of reports to ensure alignment with their needs"?

"As I said earlier, including users in the discussion is fraught with pitfalls. They do not ..."

My phone buzzed loudly and persistently.

"I see you did not mute your phone at the start of our meeting," said Berdina, clearly annoyed.

"My apologies. I thought I had done so," I mumbled as I checked the caller ID. It was Sergiu. He wanted to see me in his office right away.

I stood up and collected my papers. "I'm sorry to have to cut this short so abruptly," I said. "My manager has requested my immediate presence. I'm sure you understand."

Berdina stood up and nodded. "It was nearly time for us to end the meeting anyway. I hope this has helped whatever it is you are doing. I'm still not sure I understand why we are meeting, based on what you've told me so far."

I ignored her question. There was nothing more she could do for me. She had confirmed much of what I had expected.

"You have been very gracious with your time and your knowledge," I said. "I will be sure to show you the results of my project once I have assembled all the elements."

"Very well," she said. "That's it then. Be seeing you."

Tips that would have helped Chris

If you are unsure, ask. Ignorance is no crime

If you fail to get the information you needed, or to fully understand what is expected of you, because you are afraid of seeming ignorant or uniformed, then you will get exactly what you deserve. Do not be afraid to ask for clarity or confirmation on important items, even if you think you can guess or figure out what the answer should be.

Talk to the people who know

When a leader won't meet with you and pushes you off onto one of their staff members, don't treat it as a failure. If you are looking for understanding on how something actually works, you are much better off with the people who use it on a day-to-day basis. They are in a better position to give you the unvarnished truth, both good and bad. Remember that the majority of a leader's role is to make decisions based on conflicting choices that maintain alignment with the organization's goals. Their understanding of the operations often does not go below the conceptual level.

Governance belongs in the big tent

Governance must include representation from all involved parties, including the users. They may be ignorant of the technology or the available alternatives. However, the one thing they are not ignorant of is their needs, and the impact of changes on the delivery of services to meet those needs. Too often, even the best governance groups include only a knowledgeable few from IT. This is wrong. It is a throwback to an outside-in view of the relationship between IT and the users, where IT, in its infinite wisdom, retreats into its sacred lair, produces an answer, then through their benevolence, offers that solution to those users they deem worthy. It's an approach to the IT-user relationship that became outdated when people stopped using punched cards.

CHAPTER 9: WHISPERS IN THE HALLS

Both Art and Molly were in Sergiu's office when I got there, and judging by the conversation, they were deep in discussion. I knocked on the wall at the entrance, and everyone turned toward the door. As soon as they saw me, they stopped speaking.

"We can continue this later," said Art.

Molly nodded, and Sergiu said, "Whatever you feel is best is fine with me. Just set up some time with my admin."

I waited just outside the office as Art and Molly walked past.

"Hi," grinned Molly. "Great to see you again." I nodded and smiled.

Art walked by and made strong eye contact, but said nothing.

Once they were gone, I stepped into Sergiu's office.

"Please close the door and have a seat," he said.

Closing the door, I quickly settled into a still-warm chair on the opposite side of Sergiu's desk.

Sergiu leaned back in his chair and said, "We have to have a difficult conversation."

"What do you mean"? I asked, full well knowing that simple phrase was corporate speak almost everywhere for you're going to get punished for something by your manager. In my case, where I was on a PIP already, it had some ugly connotations.

"You're half way through the time allotted for you to successfully complete your PIP. Because of that, and because I am new here, I've been collecting feedback about your progress on your PIP from other leaders and your peers. To be blunt, the message back has not all been positive, and it is my duty to alert you that unless you improve your performance, you will not successfully complete your PIP, and may be asked to find some other organization in which to become successful."

I tried very hard to keep the emotion out of my voice and conduct the conversation objectively, as if we were simply talking about the weather. This was not a time to show weakness.

"Really? Who has expressed concern that I am not meeting the objectives laid out in the PIP"? I pulled the list of items in my PIP from my folio and began reading them, while citing examples of what I was doing to meet each of them. Doing that wasn't too hard, as each had been written so broadly, and in such vague terms, that any given behavior could meet or fail their requirements, depending on the attitude of the reviewer.

"I'm sorry, but I can't reveal that. The feedback was given to me in confidence, and I will not violate the spirit of that understanding. It could create a situation where you might pressure them to change their viewpoint."

I wondered who it might be, but with Art here just a few minutes ago, I didn't have to think very far. He was the only one close enough to my work to be able to form an opinion on it, based on actual experience.

"Can you at least tell me which areas of the PIP you're getting negative feedback about"?

Sergiu shook his head. "Sorry. It might allow you to identify the source. I am concerned you are taking this all wrong. It's not personal. Everyone here, from leadership to your peers, is committed to helping you complete this PIP successfully. We're all working hard to help you grow and become a better employee for the company. You do want that, don't you"?

I nodded, "Of course I do. It just would be a little more helpful for me if I knew where I was doing well, and where I was falling down."

"I think you are missing the point," said Sergiu. "The PIP is a totality of effort. Simply going down the list and cherry-picking some of the items, will not get you a passing grade, nor will simply complying with the letter of the document. The spirit of the effort is as important as the individual items."

I nodded, and thought to myself that what he really meant was how you did on the items they had called out, had nothing to do with whether or not you survived the PIP. It all had to do with whether or not they liked you, or you fit in with their group. I secretly hoped that Lee was failing miserably at his new role, as recompense for doing this to me.

"I think I understand," I said in my most humble voice. "I have only a few weeks to prove my abilities to you and the rest of the organization through my actions. Given that, is there any other advice you can give me before I get back to work"?

Before he could respond, Art walked back into the office, without so much as a knock or an introduction. He looked at Sergiu, then at me, and asked, "Are you ready to go"?

I looked back at Sergiu, but he started talking to Art. "I think we are done here. Yes, Chris is ready to go."

Turning back to me, Sergiu said, "Art will be taking you to meet with Dylan. He is the senior director of a field-based team that is one of the major users of IT services. While his team receives many IT services that are critical to their success, he doesn't directly receive KPI information regarding the service desk. However, his organization is extremely dependent on it ... probably more than any other team right now. This additional information should help you complete your PIP successfully."

"Yeah," snapped Art. "So pay attention to what he says."

I followed Art, but for the life of me could not figure out how listening to this user could have any impact on whether or not people in IT thought I should stay. I was beginning to wonder if they thought I was stupid enough to believe what they were saying, instead of what they were doing.

"This doesn't make any sense," I said. "This guy, Dylan, wouldn't even know a KPI if it bit him. All he wants is to meet his business objectives. I get that. What I don't get is why he should even waste any time with us talking about KPIs. If I were him, I'd want to be focused on the things that mattered to my pocketbook – meeting my organization's business objectives."

"Looks like I'll have to educate both of you," said Art. "Or maybe just you, if Dylan has any smarts about him."

"Art, give me a break. You're not the only one who knows anything here."

Art just held up his hand and waved me off. Art was smart, but all of that knowledge seemed to have been turned into the false confidence that everything he believed was the only truth.

I knocked on Dylan's door, but Art didn't wait for a response, he just barged right in and immediately sat down across the desk from Dylan. Dylan's office was somewhat like Lee's had been. It had photos and awards across the walls, and an excellent view of the greenway surrounding the building. The furniture was wood, not metal, and the lighting had all been converted to incandescent from fluorescent. It looked much more like a high-end home office than the stark, harshly lit corporate standard with its metal furniture, and all the personality of an institutional detention center.

Moments after he sat down, Art was moving items around on Dylan's desk, so there was enough space to lay out his notebook and papers. He left me standing in the doorway, stunned. This was not how you treated a director, especially a director whose team consumed a tremendous amount of IT services. Actually, consumed wasn't a strong enough word. Dylan's team was dependent on the information the IT organization provided, in order to react to market changes and customer feedback, in as near as real time as possible.

"Well, are you coming," snapped Art. "Or do you plan to make Dylan wait all day for you to decide you are in the mood"?

Dylan looked up from the stacks of folders and piles of papers that littered his desk. "I only have 15 minutes for you two, and you just used one of those minutes. Sit down, and let's get going."

I was tired of being pushed around by Art, and everyone else who yelled louder. I was taking charge this time. I walked up to the desk and stood beside Art. "No thanks. We don't have time. I'll stand."

Dylan stopped and looked up from his desk with a puzzled expression on his face. It only lasted for a moment, and then he stood up too. "Good. What do you need from me"?

For once Art seemed to not have a snappy comment. In fact, he looked kind of lost … the only one sitting in the room.

"IT provides you with a long list of services, correct"?

"Yes," said Dylan. "Our applications allow customers to track and manage … "

I interrupted. "A laundry list is not important at the moment. We can get that without taking more of your time. We're here to talk about the service desk. We are in the process of revising our Key Performance Measures."

"Fine," said Dylan. "But what's important to my organization is availability. We bill customers for service. It is a major component of revenue for the company. So if you don't provide it for us, then we can't bill it."

"I understand," I said. "So you want people on your team to get immediate response when they call the service desk, and be off the phone as quickly as possible"?

"Not at all," said Dylan.

Now I was confused.

"We don't care how long the phone rings before they pick it up. We don't care how long we are on the phone working out the answer."

9: Whispers in the Halls

"What is important to you"? asked Art.

"Our customers want issues resolved, without a lot of effort on their part," said Dylan. "We want the same thing. We want resolution. I don't want my people wasting time calling back over and over again, trying to get things resolved, or figure out where they are. The easiest way to do that is to get it resolved on the first call. Why can't you commit to doing that"?

"Well we want that too," I said. Trying to paraphrase some of Art and Sean's earlier comments, I said "The difference between a 10 minute and a 10 hour resolution can be dependent on a variety of difficult to manage factors. Sometimes the difference can simply be due to whether or not it happens on a weekend, or a weekday. We want our KPI measures of accomplishment to reasonably reflect the reality of the situation."

Dylan scowled at me. "In other words, you won't commit to a first call resolution performance level because you are afraid you may occasionally miss it. Have you ever worked in sales, or a field office"?

I shook my head. "No."

Dylan pointed his index finger at me. "I advise you to try it out. Get some real-world experience. It will improve your understanding about the level of support the business needs from IT. In the real world, we sometimes miss our performance objectives. That's reality. When we don't perform as expected, we take our lumps and learn from it. If you want to demonstrate a high-level of performance, you don't do it by lowering the bar so it's impossible to fail. You do it by establishing tough goals and instituting improvement plans and remediations when you do stumble."

"I'll give you a piece of advice," he said. "Anytime anyone says they never fail, you can rest assured they are lying. Not only are they lying, but they've never learned anything from what they do. You learn nothing from success. Only failing gives you the opportunity to see how you could do things better."

"Thank you for your insight on that," said Art. "We truly appreciate your candor. It's clear you have a better idea of what IT needs to do to support you, than IT thinks you need to be supported."

Dylan checked his watch. "Good, because your time is up. Now get out there and get me the support I need." Dylan turned and jabbed his finger at me again. "Because the support you are providing is not cutting it. If IT can't provide us with what we need in-house, then maybe we shouldn't have IT in-house, and should look at outsourcing that function. At least then we would have some leverage to get the things we need, in order to meet our business objectives."

Dylan picked up his desk phone handset and began punching numbers into the base. "Now get out of here. I've got to go earn money, so you IT people can buy more toys to play with. At least my children thank me for them."

Tips that would have helped Chris

Make everyone part of the solution

Never be afraid to include your users in discussions on decisions that could impact delivery of services to them. You may get a lot of negative venting from your users about perceived shortcomings. You may meet some resistance from the technical teams, from their fear of having stumbles exposed outside their organization. These aren't uncommon. Your service solutions will become more user focused. Users will be happier with the service and how it is delivered because they will have feelings of ownership in the solution.

Focus on the most important things first

Frustrated users will ask for a multitude of things, in an attempt to find something that will help them reach their objective, much like a drowning swimmer might grasp small branches in a futile attempt to keep from going under. Sometimes it takes people a while to get to what they really want. They have so much frustration built up that they need to simply vent at you for a while.

Beware of the secret rules

Many times corrective actions, such as PIPs, have unwritten components you must also complete. You are fortunate if someone in the process alerts you. This often comes via the use of terms like "Spirit of the PIP." Sometimes you can spot them as actions where it is impossible to measure success or failure objectively – much like a poorly written goal, such as "Work better with other employees."

Try to spot these at the start of the PIP, and see if you can make them SMART (Specific, Measurable, Achievable, Relevant, Time bound). If you don't, whether you succeed or fail in your PIP will depend on how people feel about you, not how you have done.

CHAPTER 10: WHAT'S THE USE?

The three of us were jammed into Molly's tiny rental car. It was well engineered enough that there should have been plenty of room for all of us. However, I was stuck in the back seat, surrounded by bags of clothes and shipping boxes full of business documents. From my vantage, it looked like she'd skipped the hotel and was living in her car.

"Sorry for the mess," she blurted, swerving around a double tractor trailer whose wake threatened to suck our car up underneath its tires. Her gyrations sent a pile of containers raining down on me. Molly drove like her personality ... frenetic ... never staying in one spot long.

"I know it's crowded in the back seat," she said. "That's not my fault. Company policy is to rent the most inexpensive car available on long engagements. It makes sense. After all, we spend most of our time at the client's site, not driving."

"Sounds like you need to get a new employer," said Art, as he dug his fingers into the dash to hold on.

"Or maybe one that lets you stay in a hotel, instead of making you sleep in your car," I added, as I tumbled back and forth amongst the packages and piles of belongings.

"That's not fair," she snapped. "I'm on call 24x7 and have a lot of material I need access to, for which I don't have time to run all the way back to my hotel a couple of times a day. Clearly, I work for a living. I'm not so sure about you two."

10: What's the Use?

Without warning, Molly cut straight across three lanes of interstate traffic and jerked onto an off-ramp at the last possible moment, eliciting bleating horns, squealing brakes, and a creative collection of rude gestures from the other drivers.

"Do you get much hate mail from other drivers"? I asked.

"Don't worry," she said, "This restaurant will be worth the trip. I've not been here yet, but others in my firm have, and they said it was fabulous."

"Great," said Art. "I had no breakfast and I'm starved."

Molly pulled to a halt near the front of the restaurant. We quickly hustled inside and found an open table. The restaurant was busy and bustling. For a moment, I wondered if this place mimicked the inside of Molly's head – lots of energy and motion, regardless of direction.

Even though we were dressed to our company's very loose IT standards, I felt somewhat overdressed in the restaurant. I wasn't talking about everyone, just some of them. They weren't unkempt or sloppy, just too casual for work in a corporate environment. I imagined they worked for themselves, probably working out of home offices. They could have been investment advisors, bloggers, writers, or any one of a dozen modern professions. I tried to imagine what it would be like to have that kind of job. I caught myself thinking I wouldn't have to deal with all the office politics, but caught myself almost immediately. Working from home would change nothing about what I hated in my job. It would simply make it so that no matter where I was, I would be unable to escape it. Perhaps there was some value in physical boundaries between my work life and my private life after all.

Our server came up and passed out menus. In a steady, resonant voice, he said, "Our soups for today are Tuscan sun-dried tomatoes and garbanzo, or a creamy mascarpone and mushroom soup. The specials are listed inside the menus." Before walking away he said, "I'll give you some time to decide what you want."

Molly was all smiles as she scanned the menu. "I hope you like vegetarian," she said. "I'm told they have the best spinach lasagna in the city."

"Spinach," stammered Art. "Spinach is what my food eats. Surely this place can rustle me up a steak, or a burger … some real food. I can't live on roots and berries."

Molly shook her head. "Please don't embarrass me by asking for something like that, Art. If you must, I'm sure they must have some kind of tofu burger in the kid's section. Maybe you should try something like the butternut squash and pear ravioli with rosemary sauce. I'm sure you would like it, and it would be very good for you. Your body might actually thank you."

"You did this on purpose," he said. He grabbed the hot garlic flatbread the server had just delivered to the table, tore off a piece, and shoved it in his mouth. Talking while chewing, he said, "You knew you couldn't convince me to change my mind, so you thought of this to throw me off my game."

"Actually, no. I was trying to do something nice for us all," said Molly. "I thought it would be a good bonding event. I thought we could work better together if we had more shared experience. Don't you want this to be a memorable, pleasant experience? Maybe it could lead to us working better together in the future."

Art snapped back. "We're not here to learn how to give group hugs, or sing Kum Ba Yah in harmony, or become the super business improvement team. We're here because, like it or not, we need to work together on this, and get it done. Then we can all go our separate ways. Get it"?

Trying to play the role of consigliore, I asked, "Maybe we should focus on the task at hand. Where do you want to start? What do you think of our current KPIs? Art and I got some interesting feedback from Dylan on them."

I summarized the feedback Art and I had received from Dylan about what was important to the business. They were, of course, measures that we were not collecting, and much as I hated to admit it, I was beginning to believe it was exactly for the reasons Dylan had said. We were terrified of showing any errors or weaknesses ... terrified that doing so would cause an uninformed leadership team to punish us for what Dylan had called common variance ... something that he felt was not that important.

"I understand and appreciate his frustration, but I like the ones we have now," said Molly. "It's about more than just Dylan. Perhaps he is just being the usual, overly assertive field leader. When you're not used to hearing from them, their louder voices can seem to be more important than they really are. It's our job to remember that this is about the whole company. Everyone knows what these measures are, and they are used to them. If we change them, people will think there has been something wrong with the work they have been doing. That would be demoralizing, especially given how successful we've been with them so far. Nothing but green as far as you can see."

"Repeating something useless often enough doesn't increase its value," said Art. "People used to believe the world was flat. That didn't make it right."

"I think you're both missing the point. The company ... the one that pays your employer's invoices every month, has already said they don't want any customization of the SMT tool," I said. "That makes the solution very easy. Let's look at the list the tool offers, and pick the ones we like best from them."

Molly pulled out a piece of paper and began writing. "There are hundreds of KPIs the SMT tool can produce. We need to think about which ones we want." She stopped and stared at Art. "We need to identify the ones that show how efficient, or inefficient, the service desk is being managed. I think we need a report that shows the service desk performance for dropped calls, average time to answer ... you know the core things that users look to when thinking about a service desk. We can use the SMT tool to get precise measurements to the second." Molly turned to me. "I know from experience that your management will appreciate that kind of business focus and accuracy."

"Oh no you don't," said Art, wagging his finger at Molly, a gesture she seemed to recoil at. "Dylan had said the single most important concern he had about the service desk was first call resolution."

"When you have as much experience as I do," said Molly, "You know that like they say in real estate, 'buyers are liars'. Users don't know what they want. They just tell you the first thing that pops into their head, and each time it is something different. Part of our role is to look out for them, and figure out what is best for them."

Art shook his head. "If they ask us for a measure and we don't provide it, but rather provide something else instead, then we've just given them another reason to believe that IT doesn't pay any attention to them. Wouldn't it make more sense to explain to them why what they are asking for doesn't report what management needs to run the service desk most efficiently"?

Our server reappeared. "Excuse me. Would you like me to take your order now, or at least get you some beverages"?

"We still haven't decided what we want to eat yet," smiled Molly. "And we won't know what we're going to drink until we decide what we're having to eat. We want to make sure it's balanced and appropriate."

"I don't care if it is balanced, as long as it is real food, not twigs and berries," said Art.

Molly scowled at him.

The server seemed to ignore Art's snide remark and said, "Waiting to order your beverage until you decide what you want to eat is quite proper. Try to think of your entire meal, including beverage, as a complete whole. That way you will get the maximum value from your food. It would no more make sense to order your beverage without knowing what you are going to eat, than it would to begin a journey without knowing where you are going. I'll be back in a few minutes. Please take your time."

Molly pushed a paper napkin across the table to me. It contained a sketch of a KPI report with measures, charts, and performance guidelines.

"This is where we should start. Know where you want to go and it makes the whole trip easier. We want a report that looks like this, so the question then becomes a simple one. Which canned KPIs will give us what we need"?

Art leaned over and looked closely at it. "This is an interesting approach. Perhaps ..."

I cut him off. What the server said had triggered an idea in my head. We were looking at this backwards. The purpose of the KPIs wasn't to build the nicest report; it was to help manage a business objective. That was our true goal.

"Wouldn't it make even more sense to start out with what the objective is we're trying to check on first, rather than how we want to report"? I asked. Both Art and Molly stopped and stared at me. "I'm just saying that if we start out focused on what the business goal is that we're trying to track, then we'll have a better chance of meeting Dylan's, and our, needs, than if we start out worrying what our reporting will be."

Molly shook her head. "We get graded on how the output meets the needs of the company. If the reporting doesn't provide the measures people want, we have failed."

"Sorry, Chris," said Art. "Nice try at showing some intelligence for once. Unfortunately, you've set yourself up to fail. If we don't know what the output report is; what that report looks like, then how can we figure out what to measure, or if we can collect it from the SMT tool? The easiest way to do this is to start with what we want as our output, and then work backwards based on our constraints."

I shook my head and slapped both hands down on the table. "No. You've got the idea almost right, but you've confused the medium with the communication – you've confused the report with the message we want to provide. Our objective is to monitor progress towards the goal. Our whole purpose here is not to produce the best report. It's to provide leadership with the information they need to make decisions. The report is just the manner of presentation."

"If you don't know each of our user's unique objectives, how can you provide them just the relevant information? That's why you make the report so all-inclusive," said Molly.

"No. We know what they want," I said. "We've already done that. We asked them. Remember what Dylan had said. They are the ones leadership holds accountable for the success of the business. We just weren't willing to believe him when he said the only thing that mattered was first call resolution."

I poked my finger at Molly's napkin drawing. "We thought we knew better than the users. We thought we knew what they wanted better than they did, and so we got it all backwards, because we treated it like everything else we do in IT. We looked at it from the IT's perspective, from the inside out, rather than from the user's perspective, from the outside in."

I turned over Molly's drawing and began scribbling on the other side. "The first thing we should worry about is what business objective we're trying to watch. Once we know that, we can figure out how to measure the Critical Success Factors, the CSFs, necessary to achieve that objective. Once we know the CSFs, we can figure out how to collect the data, measure and analyze it. Only after we know that, should we worry about how to report on it."

I was really proud of myself. It all made perfect sense. The reason we were having so much confusion and difficulty putting it all together, was that we were going after the wrong thing ... we were looking through the wrong end of the telescope. It was a great piece of thinking, and more importantly, it was the right approach for supporting the business.

Molly frowned and said, "I'm sorry to tell you this, Chris, but you are wrong. Art is right. I'm excited by your enthusiasm. It is a good try on your part, but you are all mixed up here. It's impossible to do what you want to do. There are too many unknowns."

We argued all through lunch. The discussion got so heated that Art even ate his tofu chili without a single, rude comment. While we still weren't in agreement, I knew by the time I crawled into the tiny backseat of Molly's car for the trip home that the event had been a success. We may not have achieved Molly's goal of additional bonding, but I was convinced now that what I had proposed was the right way to build our KPIs.

The only issue was, I still hadn't completely convinced Art and Molly. Without their positive reports to Sergiu, I was doomed to fail my PIP.

Tips that would have helped Chris

Start at the end, not the beginning

Determining how to properly establish a KPI is a little like deciphering a paper maze. Most people start at the beginning and struggle to reach the goal. The easiest way is to start at the center and work backwards to the beginning. Likewise with KPIs, start with the business objective you want to measure achievement towards, and work backwards. Start with the objective, then figure out what needs to be measured to track that. Only then do you consider how to collect the data. After you know how to collect the data, then you can figure out how to report it. By their nature, most KPI related tools are sold the other way around. They focus on the reports that are included in the tool, without even addressing what business objective they support.

Fewer KPIs is usually better

Quality, not quantity, is essential when implementing KPIs. It is not uncommon for there to be an excessive number of slightly overlapping KPIs. Not only is this wasteful, but it also creates confusion when the KPIs don't exactly point in the same direction. Commercial tools tend to produce many more KPIs than you need. They do this because they need to be useful to many different types of companies. Your role is to decide, based on the business objectives, which ones should be considered KPIs, and which are merely metrics of varying degrees of interest.

Apply governance to your KPIs

Many KPI reports are full of legacy measures that may have even been useful some time ago, but are no longer of interest. Sometimes KPIs are in place because someone thought they would be interesting to measure. The worst case is when KPIs are put in place because they are easy to measure. Aside from not being KPIs, all of these will only clog up your process, consume resources, and confuse readers. The best way to avoid this is through governance and accountable KPI owners who understand that KPIs, like all other processes, have a lifecycle, and manage them accordingly.

CHAPTER 11: BRINGING IN THE DATA

Molly and I left Art back at the main building, where he had a meeting with Sergiu. I tried hard not to be nervous about that. Who knew what kind of lies he was going to spread with my boss. My only hope was to get all the help from Molly that I could, to make this project a big success.

She signed me into the service desk building, and we had just reached her office when a knock came on the door. A moment later Ahermet stepped into the room.

"Is this a good time"? he asked, in English that clearly had been taught to him by someone who spoke with an accent from Southern England.

Molly bounded up out of her chair and walked quickly over to shake his hand … a little too quickly perhaps. Ahermet stepped back, as if she were going to attack him. Molly seemed to catch herself in mid-action and stopped short of him.

"We're glad you could make it. This is a great time. We're really looking forward to having your help. Your experience with the SMT system will be an invaluable help to us."

I didn't know anything about Ahermet. He was relatively new to this office, but had been with the company for a number of years overseas. He was one of the small group of company employees who had been schooled on the SMT tool. Most of the experts were still consultants. He had been one of the first trained, and knew the system from a hands-on operational perspective.

After Ahermet had settled himself into a chair beside me, and across the desk from Molly, she tried to bring him quickly up to speed on our purpose.

"We're trying to determine an optimized set of KPIs for the service desk team to use. We want to get the most effective and useful measures. We think we know what we want. What we don't know is whether or not the necessary information can be collected. That's where we're hoping you can assist us, as you are such an expert with the system."

"You must excuse me if I am confused," he said. "We had been told that there would be no customization of the reporting or workflows from the system." He pointed at the metrics displayed on the monitors in Molly's office. "What is wrong with these measures? My experience speaking with other organizations bears out the wisdom of that choice. The more modified the system becomes, the harder it is to install updates and patches. Also, the more difficult it becomes to perform new, customized work. One organization found that after customizing for several years, nearly 80% of the time and resources associated with implementing a new customized attribute, was spent fixing things the new functionality broke. There may be some sacrifices in the short term and adjustments in expectations, but in the end it is the best path."

"It's not a question of creating new measures. It just makes more sense for us to focus on our customer's essential business objectives. We want to do that by measuring the level of achievement of those things necessary to reach those objectives," I said. "Having more measures doesn't make the results more accurate or actionable. That's why we are going to focus on some measures that track achievement of those critical success factors which are necessary to accomplish those objectives."

I slid the napkin across the table to him. It contained a list of just six KPIs. "These are the KPIs we want to focus on. They represent what our users are most focused on, and therefore what we should be focused on."

Ahermet held up the napkin gingerly. It was wrinkled and soiled, and still contained the report outline on the other side. When Ahermet started to look at the report outline, I snatched the napkin back, and scribbled over that writing, obscuring the content, before sliding it back across the table.

"Don't worry about the other side. We're just being green and trying to save paper." I pointed to my list of KPIs. "This is what matters."

Ahermet inspected the list, and looked at us with a puzzled expression on his face. "This is all? It hardly seems worth the effort. Surely we can do more for our customers."

"That's good input, Ahermet," said Molly. "Remember, it is not about quantity of data we produce. It is about the quality and usefulness of what we produce. What we need from you is whether or not these KPIs we want are available among the hundreds of KPIs the SMT tool can produce."

"Without even looking, I can tell you that this will not work," he said, pointing at two of the KPIs. "You must understand that different data is produced by the SMT tool on specific cycles. That means they appear at different times during the month. Your data measures will be out of sync with each other. They will be from different time periods."

"Do they ever overlap"? I asked.

"Of course. Each has its own natural cycle, but they don't all end at the conclusion of each month. You will not be able to produce your reports on time to meet the monthly scorecard prepared for senior leadership. How are you planning to report this"?

"That's a great and thoughtful question," said Molly. "Right now, we're just trying to see what the issues are. That's what we need your expertise for."

Ahermet nodded. "I suppose as long as no one knows about the methodology, or source of the data, you will be able to get away with it."

I shook my head. "No, we can't do that. If we're not transparent in how these measures are developed and created, people are not going to trust them. You can't get people's trust if you don't give them your trust first."

"I cannot agree with you. I know from my own experience that if the data is too complex, people ask many questions, and that is a symptom of their uneasiness with the data."

"Perhaps we can come back and visit that later," said Molly.

One of the things I was starting to notice about Molly was that while she was very affirming and encouraging in her relationships with employees, she also seemed to be afraid to have any sort of conflict or disagreement with them. She would try to persuade them, but if she couldn't convince them to her viewpoint, she would push it aside. Molly had no problem hearing the conflicting views of others. However, she was uncomfortable with the idea that leadership also means making choices between conflicting points of view. That meant that she often had to tell someone their idea was not the best choice. When it came to the grittier parts of leadership, she just seemed to avoid it. I wondered if she regularly had to fire anyone during her career, or if she had avoided it by being a consultant without any direct reports.

Molly asked, "Do you perform any verification on the data that comes in each month, to ensure it is appropriate, that there are no distortions in it that need to be corrected before the analysis begins"?

Ahermet shook his head. "SMT produces a consistent stream of data from the same sources each collection period. We validated that when the system was initially established. There is no reason to expend valuable resources verifying what we know to be good data. Besides, anything that was inappropriate would be flagged by the analysis and reporting team during their work. Our job is to get the data for analysis as quickly as possible."

"You mean there is no kind of data governance that verifies the data is approved by your team as valid for use? There is no one ensuring the analysis and reporting team doesn't waste time on potentially bad data sets"? I asked.

"I know of no governance functions involved in the data collection. Whether there is one for other sections, I cannot say. I know only of our team. As I said, our task is to deliver the data sets from SMT to the intended users ... "

Ahermet was interrupted by buzzing from his watch.

"Excuse me," he said. "Time for prayers. I must step out for a few minutes. I will be back shortly."

Ahermet quickly walked out of the door into the din of the service desk floor and closed the door behind him. When the silence returned, I turned to Molly. She must have seen my quizzical look.

"We have people from all over the world working here ...," she said. "People of many faiths and practices. We work very hard to accommodate their needs, and make them feel like they are part of an organization that respects them, and does not ask them to violate their obligations as a condition of working here. Don't worry; he will be back in a little bit."

"That's not what I was concerned about," I said. "I'm just wondering if this is helping at all. Is it adding any value to determining what these KPIs should be, and how they should work? It seems that all Ahermet does is copy files and send them on to others. He could be sending them dead fish for all he seems to know or care."

Molly gave me a disapproving look. "That's unfair. Ahermet is incented to ensure data moves quickly and efficiently to the right place, not to analyze what he is handling. That's worth quite a bit. It's even one of the KPIs."

"Why is it a KPI? If he's just moving bad data from one person to the next, where is his value-add"?

Molly scowled at me.

I shook my head and said, "I don't mean his value as a human being. I'm just trying to understand why his team moves data, instead of having a machine do it if they don't have a value add? He doesn't even seem to understand the value and importance of what he is doing. To him, it's just bytes in a file."

"Perhaps that is the problem," said Molly. "Perhaps the company ... your company," she added extra emphasis. "Perhaps your company violated the basic three-part law of leadership instruction."

It must have been clear from my expression that I had no idea what she was talking about.

"Surely you know this. When leaders assign work to employees, they owe the employees three things about the work ... three things that provide the employee with what they need to achieve expectations in a constantly changing environment.

First, "What do you want them to do"? Most leaders get that one. Second, "How do you want them to do it"? Whether it is at their discretion, or under a leader's specific direction, they need to know what is expected of them. Some leaders get that one right. Third, and this is the one most leaders never include, although it is one of the most important, "Why you want them to do it"? It's only with that context that people can adjust to changing situations to produce the required results.

"Clearly, no one ever gave Ahermet a full description of his assignment. I'm sure if they had, he'd be doing things differently, and closer to your beliefs about what he should be doing."

Molly barely had time to finish when Ahermet returned and knocked twice at the door, waiting to be invited before entering.

"Thank you for permitting my absence, Molly," he said. "It is very much appreciated, as is your sensitivity in treating others as human beings and not machines."

Molly beamed a big smile. "It is my pleasure to show respect for every member of the team. You are all highly valuable, and your work is greatly appreciated."

I interrupted her. "Ahermet, I have a question for you. What other activities is your team responsible for? I'm talking about things that are not handled exclusively by machine, but that require active involvement of your team."

"What do you mean? We are fully occupied in our work at the company."

"I'm not suggesting your team is bored or lacking work. I'm wondering if perhaps your team is occasionally overloaded, like everyone else is, and when that happens, what is your charter for top focus"?

"Ahhh, I see. My team is accountable for the ongoing support and maintenance of the SMT tool functions that provide data to the analysis and reporting teams. If there is an incident, or other issue, that could interfere with that deliverable, my team's top priority is to keep the data flowing."

"How often does that impact your production of the KPI information"?

"You should understand that our priority is on ensuring that real-time workflows are operational in the SMT tool. Those workflows are prioritized at the A level. The KPI data itself is primarily historical, and therefore is prioritized at the B level. If we are understaffed, or have other, more urgent tasks, delivery of actual data may be deferred until the workflows are restored. When that time is material, some historical data may not be distributed on schedule."

"Sounds like the short answer to my question is 'Yes,' production of the KPI information is often impacted," I said.

"That sounds perhaps a little harsh," added Molly. "I think what Ahermet is trying to say is that if there is a concurrent A level issue, or a shortage of resources, then the KPI information may be delayed." She turned to Ahermet. "Isn't that correct"?

Ahermet nodded. "You are most correct. The KPI information is never more than a few weeks late, and it is always produced. When it is delayed, through no fault of my team, we simply repeat the old data until the new data is available, so there will be no gaps. Once the more recent data is available, we use that. Anyone who looks at the data will immediately know the situation, just by comparing the report data with prior reports. Since it is historical, there is no harm. It is only for reference and historical records."

I shook my head. "Unfortunately, that's not true. That KPI information is used by leadership to make real-time decisions on key business objectives. The data may be historical, but it drives real-time assessments and resulting actions. So any delay at all may be damaging."

Ahermet frowned. "The company leadership should not be relying on that data to make those kinds of important decisions. I urge you to let them know that they cannot depend on receiving the current information, on a regular schedule, 100% of the time. Surely they cannot blame my team for shortcomings in the tool itself"?

"Don't worry," said Molly. "No one is blaming you, or your team. We're just trying to understand what is happening."

"That makes me feel much better," said Ahermet. "I do not set my priorities, and I must respond to the requests made of me and my team. I just purchased a house here, and do not wish to create any cause for me to lose my position here at the company and jeopardize my work visa. I have a family here. I hope you can understand."

I didn't say anything aloud. Inside I was glad that Art wasn't here. I could only imagine what he would say.

"Don't worry. There is no problem," said Molly. "As I said, we are just trying to understand what happens."

Ahermet looked at his watch and stood up. "I have another appointment that I must attend. I hope you do not mind if I leave now. I do not wish to be late for that meeting. Do you have any additional questions"?

Molly shook her head.

"I have all that I need for now," I said. "Thank you for your candor and trust. We will respect it. Enjoy the rest of your day."

Ahermet nodded and said, "Goodbye to you both. I wish you success in your endeavors," as he headed for the door.

Tips that would have helped Chris

Align reporting to the data, not the other way around

It is very important to collect data on its natural cycle. Some data has a natural cycle lasting a week. Others last a month. Thoroughly investigate the type of data being collected, to ensure you are not sampling data during the middle of its cycle. If you do, the information generated from it will show variation beyond what really exists, and may cause inappropriate decisions to be made. This is where governance is so very important. Properly constituted and functioning, it will ensure that the data continues to be collected in a consistent and appropriate manner.

Manage your data collection stream carefully

Data feeding your KPIs must be dependable. It must be internally consistent for any one sample period, and also consistent over time for any one type of data. Remember that data is simply shorthand for the state of reality at a point, or over a period of time. You can improve your data process by reducing human efforts in collection, and verifying data before processing it into information. Once it is processed, you can no longer determine if it is an accurate representation of reality.

CHAPTER 12: THE SIGNAL AMONGST THE NOISE

Trey had been at the company only about a year longer than I had. He'd come to the company straight out of school, and he'd flown through school. Word was that he finished a double BS in Computer Science and Data Mining in two years, and an MS in Applied Information Economics in two more. While he didn't have an extensive work history as an employee, as a graduate student, he'd consulted to a number of marketing firms, advising them on how to deal with big data – the exabytes of information they'd collected, but couldn't manipulate into useful information without choking. He definitely wasn't dumb or ignorant, but he sounded like the kind of guy who wears a pocket protector in his pajamas – dull, boring and one dimensional.

His team's job was to receive the data from Ahermet's team, analyze it, and produce the reports which were distributed within the company.

"Trey may be the face of the KPI process to the company," said Art. "But his team is simply the final step in a lengthy chain of activities. Remember, the more handoffs in a process, the greater the chance it will fail to work properly. It's not appropriate to discuss it with him today, but in the back of your mind think about what we could do to consolidate some of those process steps. We can debrief after the meeting. I'll expect your assessment so we can come to some joint recommendations."

That sounded like pure Art. Everything was a cool calculation with a bottom line ROI. Last time I'd heard people talking like that at previous companies, entire teams were eventually laid off or fired, and the survivors ordered to fill in the gaps ... or else.

As Art and I walked into Trey's cube, it was clear he wasn't the geeky introvert I had anticipated.

The walls of his cube had pictures of him racing motocross. He'd crashed his bike the first month he was working here and broken his arm. I knew because right beside the photos, on the wall of his cube, appeared to be the cast the doctors removed from his arm, which he seemed to have had sealed and mounted on a plaque, with a picture of him being loaded into an ambulance, and another of his twisted cycle. Underneath it was the date, and a quote about how things that don't kill us make us stronger. I almost laughed when I saw a picture of him surfing on vacation with his cast sealed in some kind of plastic cushion he must have devised. Somehow, I couldn't imagine his doctor approving that.

"I'm Trey," he said, as we walked in and sat down. "You must be the exterminators we requested. We've been having a terrible problem with bugs ... bugs in our software." With a laugh, he added, "Only kidding. Who is Art and who is Chris? Or should we start by asking what is Art"?

I smiled inside. Trey may have been smart and effusive – still impressed by his own cleverness, but he hadn't been around long enough to get molded into a shape consistent with the company's view of the world. Art was going to hate Trey. I could tell already.

Trey was one of the few people I'd seen in IT that used a tablet. I scanned his office and realized there were no laptops or desktops in his office. In most of the places I'd worked before, your status and bragging rights among the technical teams was based on how many different computers you were able to weasel approval for out of accounting. Here was someone whose work was totally computerized, and could reasonably justify several computers. Why was he really eschewing that computing muscle in favor of a vastly, less powerful tablet?

As Trey tapped the screen of his tablet, I asked, "Are you having problems with your laptop"?

Trey shook his head. "Everything we do is in the Cloud – all the apps and all the data. Otherwise, my team would need their own data farm to manage it, and what now takes hours to analyze, would take days. I'm only interested in the results." Trey looked up and grinned. "I don't need to overcompensate by filling my office with equipment." He set the tablet down on the desk and spun it around so we could see it.

Grids of analytical charts slowly scrolled upwards. Most were consistently green. When the rare measurement indicated performance expectations had been broken, the application paused and zoomed in on that measure, freezing it mid-screen until we pressed the continue button.

"This is very impressive," I said.

Trey shrugged his shoulders. "It's something I wrote because I wasn't happy with anything coming out of the SMT tool. It transforms the SMT output into something more useful."

"Customizing the SMT tool is not allowed. There are too many risks to the ...," I said.

"Risks to the company," said Trey. "Yes, I know. I've heard the same message. Let me ask you this. Which would you rather have, the best information available on which to base your decisions, even though it is contrary to company policy, or some data/information which may be inadequate to make a decision on, but compliant with company policy"?

"Over the long haul, the analysis says although your decisions may be based on weaker information, not customizing is better for the company," I said.

Trey snickered. "Try talking about that to senior leaders whose compensation is 80% based on the results for the quarter, rather than performance five years out."

"You didn't customize SMT, did you"? said Art.

"Smart man," said Trey. "Never touched it. In fact, we don't even use its canned reports. We get a raw data feed directly from Ahermet's team, that is the same one the SMT report writer uses. The only difference is we do a better job of making it useful to our customers. Since we don't change SMT, and we use the same data … there is no customization. We just know a better way to analyze it."

Trey spun the tablet back so it faced him. "Of course this is only one view of the information. We have a wide variety of searches that can be conducted." He paused and looked up at Art. "And for the traditionalists among us, we also provide more familiar printed documents. So what? They show the same information. They're just not as green, and take an extra day to receive."

"In all honesty," he said. "It doesn't really matter to us what we are analyzing. It's all data in the Cloud to us."

"It's not just any data," said Art. "I can understand and appreciate how the analysis techniques may not vary much. Leadership is making decisions based on the content of this information."

"It's still all numbers. As long as the feeds get to us in a timely fashion, we will meet the deadlines, and produce what people ask," he said. "That is what leadership consistently tells us they want."

"It is more than numbers," I insisted. "You may only see numbers and charts, but they are really shorthand for whether we should be hiring or firing people; starting or stopping new customer services; or potentially even outsourcing or insourcing our service desk activities."

"You're misinterpreting me," said Trey. "We have no vested interests in the results, beyond ensuring what we produce is accurate, and reflects the sensitivities of the consumers of our information."

"Who are your customers"? I asked.

Trey tapped on his tablet. An enormous list of names began to scroll down the screen. "There are a lot, aren't there"?

"Too many," said Art. "Do they all get the same information"?

Trey nodded. "There are three variations; one with mostly numbers for the workers, one with a mix of numbers and charts for the managers, and one that is all pictures for the senior leaders. The content is pretty much the same. It's all in the presentation."

Art scribbled more notes. "What about the frequency? Does that stay the same"? asked Art.

"Look, I know where you are going with this. We know that the reports should be crafted for specific audiences, the frequency should match the natural periodic cycle of the underlying processes, and we should cull the distribution lists on a regular basis. Those are some of the first things I had my team do when I got here."

Trey swiped his tablet clear and leaned across his desk. In a much quieter and subdued voice, he said, "I even had my team put some dummy information in there, to see if anyone was reading them. I went so far as to include the phrase, 'If you do not call and confirm your desire to continue to receive this report, you will be dropped from further distributions,' in the middle of the analysis of one KPI."

Art held his hand up and said, "Wait, let me guess. You got no responses, right"?

Trey nodded. "So I called them on it. I dropped one in every 10 names from the distribution list the following cycle. I even dropped 10 of the KPIs in the report."

"Did you get a response"? I asked.

"Response," said Trey. "I nearly got fired before I finished my first month here. The only people who didn't scream were those that were no longer here. At least I was allowed to drop them. Apparently, people want to get the report whether they read it or not. If they don't get it, they assume they are out of the loop on other important things too."

Art smiled and actually laughed. "Oh yeah, seen it so many times before. What about the reports showing performance expectations always being met? Did you bring that up"?

"That's a battle I still haven't won," said Trey. The frustration was clear in his voice. "I keep getting told that showing anything other than success on every occasion causes concern and doubt in the minds of our customers. Unfortunately, that's only part of the problem. No one seems to understand the concept of normal variation. It seems like every time I try to share how the KPIs are measured and created, it only creates more anxiety. So I don't do it anymore."

"Variation needs to be reduced to zero," I said. "Everyone knows that. If you eliminate variance, you provide better service. Consistency builds customer confidence."

"At what cost"? asked Trey. "It's their resources, so if they want to spend them in pursuit of something they can never achieve, well that is their business. I give the customer what they want; and they want reporting that doesn't cause them anxiety or confusion."

"Reducing variation takes resources," said Art. "The problem is that a certain amount of variance is inherent in any process, if for no other reason than people are involved. Using resources to try to eliminate that is a waste. What you want to look for is abnormal variation ... variance beyond a specific range. Your performance expectation should be a range of values, not a single point. As long as the performance is within that range, let it go."

"That sounds crazy to me," I said. "How can you possibly know what range to assign? What if it's one-time versus consistent? It sounds like a great way to let things get out of control."

Art shook his head, and then looked at Trey. "Don't they teach statistical process control in business school anymore"?

Trey chuckled. "Not really, and then most people sleep through it."

Art laughed – louder than I had heard him laugh before. "Thanks a lot, Trey. I think we get the idea of what is happening. If you can send me the current KPI report, Chris and I will leave you to your work. I think we have more than used up our appointed time with you."

"No problem," said Trey, as he swiped his fingers across the face of the tablet. "It should be in your e-mail any moment now."

Art stood and extended his hand across the desk to Trey. "It's been a real pleasure chatting with you today. It's really nice to find someone who actually knows what they're talking about."

"Anytime you need more information, just let me know," said Trey.

Art walked out of Trey's cube and I followed close behind him.

Art led us to the break room, and after grabbing himself a cup of coffee without even bothering to ask if I would like one, he sat down. The room was empty, and I sat down across the table from him.

Referring to his notes, Art said, "Trey's had some good education, but despite his consulting assignments prior to coming here, he really needs more experience. That's probably why he couldn't make people understand the difference between <u>expected common variation</u> and unexpected special variation. Without that understanding, he is going to be locked into over-producing reports, and helping the company continue to waste resources, trying to eliminate something better left alone for now."

"From my experience," I said. "I don't think anyone could convince our leadership of the difference. It's too conceptual, too theoretical. They don't want ranges of answers. They want simple 'Yes-No' responses. Otherwise it makes their decision-making process too complex."

"Would you bet your job on that belief"? asked Art

"What do you mean, bet my job"?

"Or better yet, would you bet Trey's job on that belief"?

I hesitated. "Yes ... Yes, I would bet both our jobs on it. I've seen enough of how decisions are made here that it doesn't matter how mathematically perfect the KPIs are, anything beyond a simple answer for a measure will be too much for them. They have too many other issues to deal with, to spend a lot of time analyzing data. They want recommendations. That's our job."

"Then what's the value Trey and his team add"? asked Art. "All they are doing is running Ahermet's data through an algorithm, and presenting it in a format defined long ago. What have they added as individuals, that an automated machine process could not"?

"That's not fair. Trey needs an opportunity to educate people and get them to understand. You can't just toss Trey and his team out on the street. Think about those people. These things take time ..."

Art cut me off. "No, time is the one thing we don't have any to waste. Decisions are being made real time, right now, that impacts the jobs and futures of everyone at the company. Think about all those people. What if leadership decides to outsource the service desk unnecessarily, based on faulty information passed on by Trey's team, and the jobs of hundreds of people vanish? Do you think about them? You should."

Art checked his watch. "I need to go meet with Sergiu. He wants an update on our progress. While I'm gone, you should spend some time collecting your thoughts, and coming up with a set of recommendations for us to present to Sergiu and his peers regarding the KPI process."

After Art left, I sat alone in the break room. Shortly after Art left, Molly walked in and poured herself a cup of coffee. It wasn't until she turned to leave that she saw me.

"Oh, hi," she said. "I almost didn't notice you there. You were being so quiet. Are you okay"?

"I'm fine. Just finished a session with Trey and Art about analysis and reporting for the KPIs. It was funny. I thought Art was going to hate Trey. Trey seemed like his exact opposite, but Art seemed to like him … until we got here, and then he started talking about him and his team like they were useless."

"Sounds like Art," said Molly. "I warned you about him. I've seen him in action before. You can never trust him at face value."

"What does that mean"? I asked.

"I call him Art the secret destroyer," she said. "You never know what he is thinking. He can be as nice as he needs to be with everyone. But every time I've seen him in a company, people lose their jobs."

"Does it make me different that he treats me like an idiot"?

Molly laughed and shook her head. "Nope. It just means he doesn't view you as a potential threat, or someone who could derail his plans. So he doesn't feel he needs to spend any energy being discreet around you. You get a deeper view into what he is thinking."

"Well, it's pretty nasty," I said.

"I don't like to say anything bad about anyone unless it is absolutely called for," she said. "Still, you should be wary of him, even if you're not a threat to him right now. He will wait for just the right time to humiliate you and your ideas in front of your managers and leaders."

"So what do I do"? I asked.

"Let's take a look at the material we've collected, and try to figure out which things he will think are the weakest or hardest to explain. That's what he'll go after. What he doesn't know is that we will be ready for him."

Molly and I began working through the material, identifying areas Art was likely to dispute. Art may have been more than a match for anyone, but with Molly's help, I was going to become more than a match for him.

Tips that would have helped Chris

It is more than just lines on paper

People want control over how their information is reported and distributed. They view it as exposing their secrets to the world. This is especially true in corporate cultures, where any signs of weakness or stumbles can be fatal; cultures that don't understand the difference between signal and noise, or common and abnormal variation. This type of culture will make it challenging to produce objective, transparent reporting of KPI achievement, without first educating people about the nature of variation.

Printing reports doesn't make the content true

It is human nature to assume that no matter how inaccurate or inconsistent the data stream is flowing into an automated system, once it is regurgitated by that system, it is somehow cleansed, correct and accurate. The old phrase "Garbage In – Garbage Out" is just as important and true now as it always was.

Reports are about communicating, not art

Sometimes people confuse making a report's information easy to understand, with making it look pretty. Eye candy is a distraction, and only disengages people from the information flow. Edward Tufte has written some excellent works on how to find the right balance.

CHAPTER 13: KNOWLEDGE WANTS TO BE FREE

"Are we waiting for Molly and Art"? I asked, as Sergiu rifled through the folders on his desk.

He shook his head. "No, this is just between you and me. We need to have an important conversation."

That didn't sound very good to me. I had brought all the information we'd collected about the service desk KPI process, on the assumption we were going to go through our progress and the next steps.

Sergiu opened the one I had prepared about service desk KPIs. "I've looked through your presentation, and I was a little bit surprised at what I read. Shifting the focus from the service desk to the entire company is quite an expansion of the scope of your assignment. That is very questionable behavior given one of your PIP tasks was to more closely follow the directives of your assignments. Are you sure you want to turn this in for my consideration"?

I had assumed that Sergiu would be impressed with my initiative. It seems that I was wrong. "After collecting the information, and speaking with the various process owners, it became clear that the issue was much broader than just the service desk. I felt I would be remiss if I simply followed orders and ignored the rest. I hoped my initiative would be appreciated."

"Hmmm, did you discuss this with the consultants, Molly and Art? They have quite a bit more experience than you do. What was their perspective"?

"Molly worked very closely with me on this. If she were here, I know she would voice her support for this work." I was sure she had my back on this. She had been a strong supporter of my work since the beginning.

"And Art"?

"I haven't seen Art in days. I don't know where he is."

Sergiu checked his calendar. "Here it is. It seems he was called back to his firm's home office for an important meeting. He'll be back in two days."

So Molly was right. He was a consultant. Who knew what his agenda really was. Well, he could stay away as long as he liked. As far as I was concerned, he could stay gone forever. "I'll check with him when he returns," I said.

"Unfortunately, there won't be time," said Sergiu.

"I don't understand." Did this mean Sergiu was going to tell me I'd already failed my PIP and this was the end?

"I've arranged for a group of my peers to review this material and provide me with their feedback. In case you hadn't guessed it, this project was part of my test of you to see if you are meeting the letter and spirit of your PIP, or if we should stop wasting your time."

"When will that be"?

"You'll be on the agenda for our monthly manager's meeting in two days. Fortunately, Art will be back for the meeting. I know he will have some feedback for the group on your presentation. He's got a sharp, analytical mind and a lot of experience."

All the better for Art to shoot me down and send me out the door with my personal effects, just because that was the way he was.

I smiled and said, "Sounds great, Sergiu. I'm really looking forward to it."

As I walked out the office door, I pondered again the wisdom of packing up my personal effects just in case.

My presentation was the first item on the meeting, and they had allotted me 30 minutes, so I needed to be focused and to the point. Fortunately, I had gone over it with Molly so many times, I now knew it by heart. I don't know what I would have done without her. If I survived this, I would owe her my job. She had done so much for me, and without any benefit to herself.

I stepped to the front of the room and stood silently, as my presentation was loaded onto the screen behind me. Around the table sat many of Sergiu's peers, Molly, Art, Sean and a few other key players in IT. There were no senior leaders or directors, so calling this a dry run was appropriate. Except in my case, it was a dry run that would have a major impact on whether or not I survived my PIP. I was just hoping that I could count on Molly to offset what negative remarks Art was planning to unload on me during the question and answer section.

The title slide of my presentation was loaded, but still I remained silent and immobile. I wanted them to focus on what I was going to say. I wanted them to be hungry for what I was about to share with them. I wanted their undivided attention, and the best way to do that was to wait right up to the point where they were about to ask when I would start, before I spoke.

Finally, I began.

"Thank you all for being here. I'm scheduled to talk about a set of recommended KPIs for the service desk. With the help of Molly and Art, and a number of other individuals, we've come to some interesting insights."

I advanced to the next slide. It had one sentence on it that described the current situation. "Our current KPIs are not helping leaders make better decisions." The slide was a little over-dramatic, but I wanted to give them the key message upfront, so they could understand where I was going. I gave them a moment to read and think about it before I spoke.

"Our entire KPI process for the service desk needs to be reassessed. I could spend this presentation talking about how, with only two primary KPIs, you can get a good assessment of how the service desk is performing – first contact resolution and cost per contact. There are others that may provide additional useful information, but they all move in tandem with these two.

The measures you are accustomed to receiving, such as how quickly a representative picks up the phone, or how long a customer is on the phone, are not that highly correlated with success in the user's eyes.

The real issue is that our KPI process for the entire company needs to be reviewed. We are producing numbers that, while accurate, have little actionable connection to the forces driving our company."

A couple of people started taking notes. That felt great. It meant they were listening. "Our KPIs are simply a long list of general purpose metrics developed by the SMT tool vendor. They are not specific to our needs."

"We cannot fall into the trap of customizing the SMT tool," said Clement, the manager of the server teams. "This was before your time, but I assure you, it was a mess. It became impossible to upgrade the previous tool, and it was constantly broken."

"I know," I said. "We cannot customize the tool for exactly the reasons you mentioned. However, giving people useless information, simply because it is what you can measure, is not much of an improvement; nor is giving people huge numbers of measures, with no actionable direction, much better. We can have both appropriate and unique KPIs of a manageable number if we are creative. All we need to do is treat the SMT tool as a data source. There are plenty of commercial applications that will provide us with much more flexibility in what, and when, we get information from the SMT tool."

"That's expensive," said Clement. "We just spent millions of dollars on the SMT tool. I know. I was on the evaluation committee. We made the right decision."

"Yes, the committee did make the right decision. I am not questioning that. I am talking about continual improvement. Let's take advantage of that decision the committee made, and get the best possible actionable information to our leaders, without worrying about whether it comes directly from a particular tool or not. Will it cost some money? Yes. Even at that cost, giving the best actionable information to leadership, regardless of the tool involved, has a very quick payback, and is easily financially justifiable. The best service management practices are not 'Fire and Forget.' They should be continually improved."

I advanced to the next slide. "Your best KPIs are those tied to a specific business or operational goal. Too many of what we are calling KPIs, are simply interesting measures. That's why we have too many. We need to focus on the significant few, not the trivial many."

Art raised his hand and said, "I have a question."

Just hearing his voice stopped me in my presentation. This was where he was going to sabotage me. Fortunately, Molly had forewarned me. I looked at her, and she nodded, as if she were thinking the same thing I was. I was prepared.

"In an ideal, academic world," said Art. "I agree that KPIs should be measured against business or operational objectives. However, we live in the real world, and many of those objectives are nearly impossible to directly measure. How can you advocate we focus on objectives we cannot measure"?

"Great question," I said. "The key is to understand that any objective has certain things that must happen for it to be achieved. These are the critical success factors, or CSFs. If you can't directly measure the achievement of something, measure the progress towards achieving the CSFs required to make it happen."

I held back a smile. This was one of the areas Molly and I had talked about. I glanced at her, and she was starting to smile.

Art wrote some notes, and then said, "Makes sense. Thank you."

I continued on through the presentation, talking about the importance of transparency, and making KPIs that are appropriate for each type of audience, and not wasting people's time on measures irrelevant to them. When I got to reporting and analysis, I paused for a moment.

"One of the reasons our KPIs need so much help, is that we've been approaching them backward. We've started with what we can report, and then tried to figure out who should get it, and then how we should analyze it, and then where to get it. We rarely connect it to a strategy or objective.

There are six things we must keep in mind when dealing with KPIs, whether they are for the service desk or the entire company, we need to consider them in a specific order, just like People, Process and Tools."

I put a new slide up on the screen.

1. Understand what the business strategy or objective is, before worrying about how to measure it.
2. Decide on how to measure the data, before worrying about how to collect it.
3. Decide on how to collect the data, before worrying about how to analyze it.
4. Decide on how to analyze the data, before worrying about what is actionable.
5. Understand what your users need to take action, before designing how you report on it
6. If at any point your KPI stops making sense, either you don't need it, or you didn't do a good job on the previous steps.

Everyone was taking notes. That was great.

The next slide was one of the more important ones. It was a key concept that would determine whether or not we could deliver a world-class KPI information system.

"We discovered that there is confusion about how performance expectations for KPIs should be set. Having a single value represent success or failure is unrealistic, unrepresentative of reality, and wastes resources. I am not going to try and explain statistical process control in this meeting. I don't even pretend to be an expert in it. At a very high level, there is an essential concept we all need to embrace. KPI measures vary over time. Variance is in, and of itself, not cause for concern. Every process has variation in it over time. That's called common variation, and is generally not worth trying to prevent or remediate. However, there are other levels and frequencies of variation called special variation, and those are where we need to focus our actions. Just as we need to focus on the significant few measures and ignore the trivial many, so must we focus on the special variations from KPI expectations and ignore the trivial common."

Mathis, the storage manager, interrupted me. "How can we possibly figure that out, much less explain it to leadership? It is much too complicated for them to understand. If we say statistical process control, they will throw us out of the room. They will think we are trying to hide any performance shortfalls."

I nodded. "Perhaps, but you have a really low opinion of them if you think they cannot understand complex ideas. We need to do a better job of helping them understand. Statistical process control has a number of proven techniques with demonstrable results."

"I used that when I worked in a car manufacturing company many years ago," Art said.

Mathis stared at Art and said, "I'm sorry to disappoint you. We do not manufacture cars."

Before Art could respond, I spoke up. "True, but IT is much more like a manufacturing company than we like to admit. I understand this may be a difficult concept for people to embrace. It may take a while to accomplish. However, in the end it will give us world-class decision support tools for our leadership. If we show them the benefits, I know leadership will embrace it, because above all else, they want to win."

I kept moving forward through the presentation until I reached the end. I was very happy. Some attendees had taken pages of notes, and I hadn't noticed a single one answering e-mail or text messages. I'd been able to grab and hold their attention. Even if they let me go right after the meeting, in my heart I knew I'd won this one.

"There are a lot more aspects to consider when developing KPIs, whether for the service desk or for the entire company. However, we only have about five minutes left. All of this material, and much more, is in the package on the table in front of you. I want to give you an opportunity to ask questions," I said. "My recommendation is that we make governance and development of KPIs ... real KPIs, the kind leadership can use to make critical business decisions ... an essential part of IT, with appropriate funding and support."

I turned off the presentation and said, "Are there any questions"?

Art spoke first, "Are you saying you want to be in charge of a KPI process team for IT"?

Molly lost her smile. This was not one of the outcomes we had anticipated.

I spoke without thinking. "At this moment, you, Molly and I have spent more time looking at this than anyone else. Although I am the only employee of the three, I'll support whatever the company wants to do. If that means I have to make it happen, fine. If it doesn't, fine. I just know that it needs to get done for the company to survive. Do you want the company to survive? I do."

Molly smiled, and I knew I had done well.

Tips that would have helped Chris

Start at the end, not the beginning

Determining how to properly establish a KPI is a little like deciphering a paper maze. Most people start at the beginning, and struggle to reach the middle. The easiest way is to start at the goal and work backwards to the beginning. The same is true for KPIs. Identify the objective you want to track, and then figure out the means and methods to do so. If you do not, you will waste time, end up with many more KPIs than you need, and many KPIs that don't apply to your objective.

Not all KPI red flags are cause for alert

When you talk about math to most people, they think about single, precise, repeatable answers. Statistics are about ranges and estimations. KPIs are statistical tools used to identify excessive variation. Some people don't realize that, and believe a single red flag is a failure. Variation is not always bad. Variation is a normal part of every process. Everyone will sometimes produce variations that result in KPI red flags that are not worth remediating. Only by using the appropriate tools and analysis, such as statistical process control techniques, can you tell if variation is simply noise in the process, or if it is truly a signal that something needs further attention.

Beware the perfect record

If you are proud of your process because its KPIs have been green for a long time, then either your performance level is set too easy, you are over-resourced, or that KPI is not well aligned with the objective. This is an extremely difficult concept for many people to learn, especially those whose roles are primarily decision making, based on presented information, such as leadership. An effective way to reach many of them, is concentrating on wasted resources. To be green all of the time requires substantial resources, yet yields little benefit compared to a few yellows and reds.

CHAPTER 14: LONG GOODBYES

I lingered in the hall outside the boardroom for a few minutes, before heading back to my cube. The door was closed, and although I could hear the muffled sound of voices, none of the conversation was intelligible ... and that was killing me.

Just a few feet away from me, on the other side of that door, a group of people were talking about all the work I had done with Molly and Art ... work that my boss, Sergiu, was presenting. His being my boss didn't give him any special knowledge of what I had come up with, beyond what he'd seen in the dry run. In fact, every time I tried to brief him on our progress, or the details afterwards, he had brushed me off. And then, despite his ignorance, he'd even had the audacity to change the presentation I'd prepared. There was no way he could possibly know the nuances and details that were in my head and not in the presentation. Because he insisted on presenting it, my work was going to look less than it really was.

That hurt my ego more than a little. The part that actually scared me, was that I was nearly at the end of my 90-day performance improvement plan. I'd done everything that had been asked of me on the plan, but apparently that wasn't enough. There was some unwritten piece to it, and no one, not even Sergiu, seemed willing, or able, to tell me what that was. Not knowing what leadership wanted me to change in order to keep my job, while not being able to find out, was driving me crazy. I'd finally decided it was some kind of escape clause, to allow them to legally fire me, and then make up an explanation afterwards. The one thing I did know for certain was that if my proposal on KPIs was turned down, my remaining tenure here would be brief. Today would probably be my last day.

The worst part was, I didn't even get the chance to succeed or fail on my own.

I was sitting in my cube, still cleaning up all my unread e-mail from the last few weeks and organizing it into categories, when a meeting invitation came in. It was from Sergiu. I hesitated for a moment. The presentation must finally be over. For him to schedule a meeting with me that quickly probably meant something had been decided at the meeting about my status.

I took a deep breath and opened the invite. I gave an audible gasp when I saw what it said. The meeting was for first thing in the morning tomorrow. The subject was, "Post PIP Assignment," and in the body of the invite was a brief comment from Sergiu.

"Congratulations on completing PIP. Meeting went very well. We need to structure your new assignment/role. Be careful what you ask for, you may get it."

I'd survived!

If I understood the body of the invite, I was going to be involved in creating a real performance measurement system across the company, or at least the service desk. This was fantastic. It couldn't have turned out better. I had to share the good news with Molly. So much of the credit went to her.

I called her office. There was no answer, just her voicemail. I tried her cell phone. There was no response there either. I was so excited, I ran out into the parking lot and headed over to the service desk building to share the good news with her. Molly didn't respond to calls from the security desk at the front door, so I had them call Jahmal, one of her supervisors. He came and escorted me to Molly's office. Jahmal stood in the doorway as I stepped into Molly's office. The chatter coming from the service desk agents on the floor was even louder than I remembered. The office was empty of any sign she had been there. All of her personal effects; her pictures, notebooks, blazer, and even laptop, were all gone. It looked like a fresh, new office just waiting for a new occupant.

"She packed up and took all of her personal effects a little while ago. You just missed her," said Jahmal. "She said she had a plane to catch, and asked her supervisors to share her goodbyes with their teams. She didn't want anyone to feel slighted because she hadn't had time to thank each of them individually." Jahmal handed me a sheet of paper. "She did send this out to everyone."

It was a printout of an e-mail from Molly to the service desk team, apologizing for her rapid departure, and thanking each of them for all of their hard work, and telling them they were the best group of people she had ever worked with.

"Thanks. That's just like her, always more concerned about her team and her people than anything else. Why did she take everything. Where was she going"?

Jahmal nodded. "Yeah, she really made this a great place to work ... always so interested in making things better for you. Too bad she didn't leave an e-mail address, so we could thank her."

I looked closer at the printed e-mail. Jahmal was right. In fact, there was no mention of our company here either. It seemed a little generic for the kind of focus she always had. Maybe she'd just done it in a hurry. Employers can be very demanding. I knew that for sure.

I handed the sheet of paper back to Jahmal, as I headed out the door and back to my building. I was more than a little nervous. Was she coming back? She had been so central to my survival here, and now she was gone. Could I really do it on my own? Would I need to confront Art, or was he leaving too?

"Going to lunch"? asked Sean, leaning over my cube wall. "Or more accurately, why don't you stop what you're doing, and you can buy us both lunch to celebrate your survival"?

I shook my head. "Thanks. You have no idea how happy I am about surviving. Normally I'd be thrilled at the idea of saving you from starving to death, but I need to finish sorting out all of these work papers from the KPI project, and I'm almost done."

Sean shook his head. "Then consider that you now owe me a lunch for missing out on this opportunity to celebrate your accomplishment. Glad you made it."

I laughed and waved him off. "Right. Now get out of here so I can finish up."

By the time I was done it was well past lunchtime, so there was no one to go with. I was not going to eat vending machine food today. I'd had too much of that over the last few weeks. I headed for the parking lot and started going through my mental list of favorite eating places.

I was out the door and part way to my car when I saw him. There was Art, pulling a rolling bag along behind him. I grinned. Despite his best efforts at crushing me, I'd survived. I had beaten him at his own game. Even though he had tried to make me fail my PIP, with Molly's help I'd survived and actually thrived. I couldn't resist the opportunity to gloat a little bit. I was in the mood for a little confrontation.

Art saw me before I saw him, and immediately stopped. He was typical Art, standing there staring impatiently at his watch as I walked across the parking lot.

"Looks like you survived," said Art. "I guess that means our proposal was approved by leadership."

"Not our proposal ... my proposal. You can't claim any credit for doing anything other than throwing rocks in the way."

"You wouldn't know a rock in your path if it hit you. Sometimes rocks in the road are nature's way of helping you around tough spots. It's the boulders you need to be wary of."

"Doesn't matter. I still beat them all," I said. I was really proud of what I'd accomplished. After the last few weeks, I was confident I could take on any challenge and succeed.

"No you didn't," said Art. "Don't ever get so arrogant you think you did. Remember this above all else ... 'No One of Us Is As Strong As All Of Us.' What we accomplish we do with the insight and support of those all around us. You're no different."

"Really, and what about those who work to make it fail? You know who I'm talking about, don't you? What happens to them"? I stared straight through Art.

"If you succeed despite them, you get stronger and more capable, and have confidence earned the hard way. And they pack up their things and move on to another situation, or another time."

I looked down at Art's rolling luggage. "So I noticed."

Art shook his head and started walking again. I refused to let him go like that. I wanted him to admit what he had done, and that I had beaten him at his own game.

We stopped beside a small rental car, nearly identical to the one Molly had driven. Art opened the trunk and lifted his bag up with a grunt, before tossing it in. Rather than closing the trunk, he opened his bag and rummaged through the documents inside. He pulled out a sheet of paper.

"Chris, do you know the meaning of the word hubris"? he asked.

"Of course I do," I said. "It's being blinded by pride."

Art shook his head. "Where is a good classical education when you need one? That's close. It's excessive pride or arrogance from an overestimation of one's capabilities or competence."

He handed me the sheet of paper. "No one in your company will show you this. It is confidential. But I think you have a need to know. I think it will only help you become better."

I scanned the document. It was a copy of Molly's recommendation to Sergiu on my performance, dated last night. I couldn't believe what I was reading. She called my work sub-standard, with no regard for the needs of my company or users, that I had failed to gain the support of the teams involved, and that I had plagiarized much of the presentation from work that she and her consulting firm had produced … work she had shared with me, despite her firm's policies against doing so, in the hope that it would teach me how to develop such a plan of my own design, not steal theirs. She took credit for the entire KPI plan and presentation. She summarized it by saying that not only had I failed the elements of my PIP as described to her by Sergiu, but that I should be dismissed immediately to minimize further damage to my company from my ineptitude.

I shoved it back at Art. "This is a fake. I know you are capable of low things, but this is beyond sleazy, even for you. Why would you do this? Do you hate losing that much"?

"Sure I loathe losing. You don't understand what's going on here. This wasn't about winning or losing. It was about doing the right thing."

"That's impossible. Molly would never give this kind of feedback to Sergiu. You on the other hand ... This is what I expected from you."

"Don't flatter yourself. You're hardly worth my time." Art reached back into his bag and passed me another sheet of paper. It appeared to be his recommendation to Sergiu. I scanned through it.

"This is kind of harsh, too," I said.

"It's realistic. It simply says what I've been saying all along. You're ignorant of many things, and sometimes a little slow on the uptake. However, you do learn from experience, and I saw you become willing to stand up for what you believed in ... to advocate in plain terms for what you believe to be right. Which is why I recommended Sergiu take you off the PIP and put you in charge of the entire KPI process. That's a process that needs an independent thinker who isn't afraid to stand-up for what they know is right. Every company needs those kinds of employees. If he hadn't kept you here, I'd have told my firm to find a place for you, because you've become the kind of person we hire."

"Why would Molly write such a letter about me. We were good friends, while you and I ... "

Art cut me off. "We're not good friends, but we do accomplish our mutual objectives. Unlike Molly, I try hard to work with others. It is not my strength, so I try extra hard to do so in my own way because I know my limits. Molly doesn't really work well with others. She is very good at getting others to trust her, and then using those people to achieve her objectives."

"I don't believe you," I said.

Art slammed the trunk closed.

"Suit yourself," he said. "Before you come to a final decision, follow the breadcrumbs. Who benefits if Molly's recommendations are enacted"?

I opened my mouth, but before I could speak, Art said, "It's a rhetorical question. The answer is she and her firm. She remains, and her firm staffs the KPI function and exercises substantial influence over your company, by controlling the data your leaders use to make decisions. That gives them the leverage to expand their consulting engagement with your company. If my recommendation is accepted, I move on to another assignment, and you achieve an increased level of responsibility and stability."

I stood there silently as Art got into the car and started it up. He lowered the driver's side window.

"Anything else? I have a plane to catch," he said.

"Well, at least I don't have to believe that you are secretly a nice guy," I responded with a smile.

"Don't ever think that for an instant, because I'm not. Oh, and in case he didn't tell you, Sergiu is having us come back in a year to provide an outside assessment of the status of the KPI process. You've got a lot of work to do, and my firm will probably send me. So you better get busy, because I expect the best. And if you are not up to my standards by then, I will kick your hind end all over the building."

Art rolled the window up, and without even a wave, drove off.

I was standing there silently for a moment, trying to process everything, when a car horn bleated just behind me. It was Sergiu.

"Are you okay"? he asked.

I nodded. "Just thinking about my new assignment."

"Sorry for having to use a meeting invite. Jessica had me in another meeting, so the only way I could share your success with you was via the invite. The meeting with Jessica is finally over and I'm famished. Are you interested in lunch? I had a vegetarian place recommended to me. It's supposed to be fantastic."

"Did Molly tell you about it"?

He nodded.

"I was there with her. I think we can find something better."

"Really"? he asked. "Okay. Hop in and let's get going."

"Great, I've got some more ideas about KPIs, and I'd really like your feedback."

Tips that would have helped Chris

Everyone has an agenda

Agendas are not bad. Everyone has them. Agendas are simply a path to obtain the goals you want to reach. Understanding the agendas of the people you work with is very important. Always assume positive intent. Understand that what is positive for them, may not be positive for you. The crime comes not when they have a different goal, rather when they pretend you have the same goal, to take advantage of you.

Style is not intent

Sometimes you will work with people whose style is the antithesis of yours. Don't assume that means they are opposed to you, or your agenda. Pay less attention to how they present themselves than you do to what they do, even if working with them seems painful in the short term. When in doubt, follow the benefits trail. Who benefits the most if different events occur? Many very successful businesses have been created by people with opposite styles who shared the same objectives.

Don't expect everyone to be as excited about your success as you are

When things go well and you achieve your objective, you have every right to be excited and share that with those around you. While they will be happy for you, if you expect them to be just as excited, you may be disappointed. It does not mean they are jealous or upset with you. It is just that your success is more personal to you. This applies to everyone around you, from your peers to your manager. The closer their goals were aligned with yours, the more excited they will be. Set your expectations accordingly, and learn how to celebrate your own success.

ITG RESOURCES

IT Governance Ltd sources, creates and delivers products and services to meet the real world, evolving IT governance needs of today's organisations, directors, managers and practitioners.

The ITG website (*www.itgovernance.co.uk*) is the international one-stop-shop for corporate and IT governance information, advice, guidance, books, tools, training and consultancy.

www.itgovernance.co.uk/itil.aspx is the information page on our website for ITIL resources.

Other Websites

Books and tools published by IT Governance Publishing (ITGP) are available from all business booksellers and are also immediately available from the following websites:

www.itgovernance.eu is our euro-denominated website which ships from Benelux and has a growing range of books in European languages other than English.

www.itgovernanceusa.com is a US dollar-based website that delivers the full range of IT Governance products to North America, and ships from within the continental US.

www.itgovernanceasia.com provides a selected range of ITGP products specifically for customers in the Indian sub-continent.

www.itgovernance.asia delivers the full range of ITGP publications, serving countries across Asia Pacific. Shipping from Hong Kong, US dollars, Singapore dollars,

Hong Kong dollars, New Zealand dollars and Thai baht are all accepted through the website.

www.27001.com is the IT Governance Ltd. website that deals specifically with information security management, and ships from within the continental US.

Toolkits

ITG's unique range of toolkits includes the IT Governance Framework Toolkit, which contains all the tools and guidance that you will need in order to develop and implement an appropriate IT governance framework for your organisation. For a free paper on how to use the proprietary Calder-Moir IT Governance Framework, and for a free trial version of the toolkit, see *www.itgovernance.co.uk/calder_moir.aspx*.

There is also a wide range of toolkits to simplify implementation of management systems, such as an ISO/IEC 27001 ISMS or an ISO/IEC 22301 BCMS, and these can all be viewed and purchased online at *www.itgovernance.co.uk*.

Training Services

IT Governance offers an extensive portfolio of training courses designed to educate information security, IT governance, risk management and compliance professionals. Our classroom and online training programmes will help you develop the skills required to deliver best practice and compliance to your organisation. They will also enhance your career, by providing you with industry-standard certifications and increased peer recognition. Our range of courses offers a structured learning path, from foundation to advanced level, in the key topics of information security, IT governance, business continuity and service management.

ISO/IEC 20000 is the first international standard for IT service management and has been developed to reflect the best practice guidance contained within the ITIL framework. Our ISO20000 Foundation and Practitioner training courses are designed to provide delegates with a comprehensive introduction and guide to the implementation of an ISO20000 management system and an industry-recognised qualification awarded by APMG International.

Full details of all IT Governance training courses can be found at *www.itgovernance.co.uk/training.aspx*.

Professional Services and Consultancy

As IT service management becomes ever more important in organisations, the development of a management system that can be certified to ISO/IEC 20000 becomes a greater challenge.

IT Governance has substantial real-world experience as a professional services company specialising in IT GRC-related management systems. Our consulting team can help you to design and deploy IT service management structures, such as ITIL and ISO20000, and integrate them with other systems, such as ISO/IEC 27001, ISO22301, ISO14001 and COBIT®. Like ITIL itself, we pride ourselves in being vendor neutral and non-prescriptive in our mentoring approach, transferring the knowledge that you need to document, challenge and improve.

For more information about IT Governance consultancy for IT service management, see: *www.itgovernance.co.uk/itsm-itil-iso20000-consultancy.aspx*.

Publishing Services

IT Governance Publishing (ITGP) is the world's leading IT-GRC publishing imprint that is wholly owned by IT Governance Ltd.

With books and tools covering all IT governance, risk and compliance frameworks, we are the publisher of choice for authors and distributors alike, producing unique and practical publications of the highest quality, in the latest formats available, which readers will find invaluable.

www.itgovernancepublishing.co.uk is the website dedicated to ITGP, enabling both current and future authors, distributors, readers and other interested parties to have easier access to more information, allowing them to keep up to date with the latest publications and news from ITGP.

Newsletter

IT governance is one of the hottest topics in business today, not least because it is also the fastest moving.

You can stay up to date with the latest developments across the whole spectrum of IT governance subject matter, including risk management, information security, ITIL and IT service management, project governance, compliance and so much more, by subscribing to ITG's core publications and topic alert e-mails. Simply visit our subscription centre and select your preferences:

www.itgovernance.co.uk/newsletter.aspx.

CPSIA information can be obtained
at www.ICGtesting.com
Printed in the USA
LVOW04s1108300816
502474LV00018B/176/P